MY PAIN IS MY

PURPOSE

Your Situation is Not Your Destination

TOYONDA SIMONE

KJV Scriptures: The Holy Bible; Published by D & H Brother's Industries Co., LTD – ISBN 9789868522312

Printed in the United Stated of America

First Edition: August 2018

Published by Queens Stay Busy | www.ToyondaSimone.com

Formatting/typesetting by Ebony Nicole Smith | www.EboonyNicoleSmith.com

ISBN 13: 978-0692101353

ISBN 10: 0692101357

Printed in the United Stated of America

Dedication

I dedicated this book to my kids. I pray that in life you understand your purpose. Take time to get to know God and everything will be ok. The struggle I went through in life was built for me to become a strong mother, a friend, and a supporter to you three.

Kamitra, Destiny, and Wayne III, life is going to take you through ups and downs and I want to be there for every single up and every single down. I may not be able to get you through them all, but just do this one thing for me, stay connected with God. Keep the connection with Him, and you three will be just fine.

In this life, it's a guarantee that you will run into some real tough times, but when you feel your prayers are not being answered or if you ever feel alone, just remember these words from me, faith prayer, and Push. Have faith. Take it to the Lord in prayer. And Pray Until Something Happens.

On your good days, pray and thank God so that when you need to pray on your bad days, it's already familiar to you. I am always praying with you and for you through the power of a praying mother.

Love always, your mother

Toyonda Simone

Contents

Acknowledgments

First, I would like to give thanks to God, because without Him I could not have done any of this. God gave me the strength to write this book and the courage to continue in life.

To my kids, Kamitra, Destiny, and Wayne, you three are my motivation and my reason for pushing for better. I love y'all infinity.

To Carlos, my soon to be husband, thank you for understanding me and loving me for me and not for what the world portrayed me to be. I love you, my best friend and my partner.

To my sister in Christ, my friend, Geralda Larkins, thank you for being my mentor and my friend. God placed you in my life and that was an extra bonus for me. Thank you and I Love you dearly.

To my mother, Betty Bryant, for raising the strong woman that I am. Thank you, Mom. I love you.

To my siblings, Brandi, Neal, Chris, Abraham, and Victor(rip), I love y'all dearly.

Thanks to my father (stepfather), for being a father figure in my life.

Thanks to my dad, Willie Howze (RIP).

To my nieces and nephews that are more like siblings to me, thank you all for being who you are.

Thank you to my special friends, women that have been there through thick and thin. You guys were there when things got tough and when I needed to hear the truth no matter how it may have hurt or helped me. Shacola, Quieta, Lisa, Keirra, and Ronnie, I couldn't ask for a better group of loving women.

Let's not forget about my purpose pusher, Lashawn Spry, I love you, girl.

TOYONDA SIMONE

I never understood why I had to endure so much pain throughout my years. When I had been through enough and began to analyze my life, I realized that my pain wasn't just for me, my pain was a part of God's purpose for my life. Your pain is your purpose. Throughout your journey, you will be destined to go through some things. It may sound crazy, but your pain is not for you, it's the purpose of your life.

We go through things to be a blessing for someone else. God gives His battles to His strongest. He wants to use you to do His work. He wants this world to be more like Him and less like us. So, today I present to you my life, knowing that my life was made to inspire others to get through what they have to go through.

You have to go through to understand the purpose of your own life. Everyone is inspired by someone, somehow. Stop, pay attention, and understand your[i] pain. Start understanding you for who you are destined to be.

This is my story. This is my truth.

This is how my pain became my purpose.

Introduction

I started writing this book about two and a half years ago. Not knowing where to start or what to do, I began keeping a journal of everything that happened in my life. I journaled the hurt, the pain, and the inaccurate perceptions people had of me. I wrote about not understanding where my life was going, and about not knowing who I could trust, who I could depend on, or even what I could depend on. And I took note of everything and everyone that was, or was not, fit for my life. This alone lets you know that I was lost in a world of confusion.

I was a friend and a partner to everyone who needed me, there for what they wanted of me. However, I never once consulted God about what He had for me or what He needed or wanted of me. I played every role that I could for others, not realizing that those others, those people around me, were not supportive of me. I never played the role God had set aside for me, and I never realized that had I played His role, He would have been supportive of every move I made. I was trying to fit in with the world, but where I was trying to fit in was not where I belonged. I belonged with God and on God's path for my life.

As a result of doing my own thing, I'm sure my life was harder than it had to be. Everyone knows that when the shoe fits, you wear it and when it doesn't fit, it's very hard to force it. I was forcing my life in one direction while God had plans for me in another one. That wasn't how my life was supposed to be, I wasn't supposed to be forcing the fit. I was supposed to have it all together and I didn't. Some people would say that a perfect life is a life with no worries. I agree. That perfect life should have been true for me. It wasn't.

Even though I was on my own path and not on a Godly track, I wasn't completely alone in the world. My family was there. They were a supportive family, they had my back no matter what situation I was in. Whatever decision I made, they never tried to stop me. They allowed me to choose my direction with no lectures from them. They allowed me to select my own way because they wanted the best for me. But what they didn't understand was that I was making decisions based on the lives of others, or rather, based on the movements of others. Then again, it all could have been part of God's set up. It could have been a part of His plan to allow me to make bad decisions so that I could learn from my mistakes and so that I could learn to depend on Him.

Because of my family's level of support, I wasn't fully aware of the fact that the decisions I'd made weren't in my best interest. It was as if my family was pacifying me through life, knowing deeply, or maybe not knowing at all, that I was headed for destruction. I was the child that would sell you something bad but would make it seem so good that you either believed me or just watched me to see how the plan played out.

People believed I had that perfect life because my family cared so much about me and desired the best for me. My loved ones did any and everything for me to make sure I was comfortable, but one thing the outside world, and my family, didn't know was that there were pieces of me that were missing. Broken pieces, pieces that, still today, have the ability to stop my growth in life if I let them.

The shattered pieces that stunted my growth back then were, not having my biological father, having the only father figure in my life die, and having a lack of guidance. In an attempt to replace the broken pieces with found pieces that I thought had been missing, I would travel down a road I wasn't prepared for, a road that was more grown than I was ready for. As a result, I became an adult at a very young age.

It didn't seem as if many people understood my life, and at one point I couldn't even understand my life. But when realization set in, I came to the conclusion that no one would *ever* be able to understand me and my life. Why? Because it wasn't for them to understand. And if I didn't consult with God and get connected with Him, I would never be able to understand my life either.

From the outside looking in, my life looked like a series of bad decisions accompanied by trial after tribulation. But what I learned when I became more mature in God was that my life had been one big growth spurt that led me directly to Him.

It wasn't until I became connected with other women that I would find I wasn't alone in my struggles and that there were many similarities in our respective lives. For the most part, the difference between me and them at that time was that they had a connection with God. I didn't. I never gave up on God, but at a certain point in my life, which will be discussed later in the book, I did not think God heard my cries. I became disappointed because things were no longer going my way. In reality, it was all really just a test of my faith.

When I finally reached a place where I had acknowledged God's presence in my life, I challenged myself daily. I did my best to learn what my purpose was and what His plan for my life was. But I was still a little frustrated because throughout the years of writing this book, I was seeing others accomplish their writing goals, seeing them become published authors and doing great things while I seemed to be at a standstill.

I was baffled about why I didn't seem to be progressing when I'd had the plan for my book and for what my book would be about years ago. I'd had my own plans for my whole life, so I couldn't see any other way. But I learned over time and through experiences with God that God had plans as well. He positions everyone in life, and when it is your time to walk in your purpose, everything will all come naturally.

Through it all, I learned that my season is not determined by other people's seasons. Everyone has their own season in life, you just have to know when it's your season. God's timing is not our own timing, things don't move because we want them to move.

When we wonder or question why things are not moving the way we think they should move, it is almost always because we are just not ready. God will position you only when He knows you're ready. However, no matter the time or the place, always remember that whatever position is for you, or no matter what's in your heart, it will not happen in your timing. It will always happen in God's timing.

Pastor Geralda Larkins, a friend/sister/mentor of mine was introduced to me at a time when I needed God the most, a time we will discuss later in the book. Pastor Larkins told me that I had to get through my journey in order to get to where I wanted to be. At first, I didn't understand, but as time went on I began to get it.

What she was telling me was that I was still in a hurt place and that I couldn't write or even motivate anyone if I had not healed enough for my own testimony. So, I reflected on what I was going through and realized that I was still fighting. And the continued fighting would only be a hindrance because I had to be totally healed in order to start what I had in my heart to do, in order to be an inspiration and a motivation for others.

Pastor Larkins also told me to continue writing down whatever God put in my spirit, that it would all come to me, and that the book would be great. However, in order for that greatness happen, I had to allow some things to take place in my life so that I could understand what she was telling me. I had to complete my journey to fully appreciate the greatness of my journey. I had to live out my destiny in order to be an inspiration to others as they lived out their destiny as well.

I remember lying in my bed on August 17, 2017 at 1:42 a.m., wondering when I'd know that it was my time. I was stuck in confusion, wondering what my purpose was and worrying about knowing what God's plan for my life was. I began the introduction to my book, stopped focusing on others, and meditated on God, knowing that He would answer me. During this time was when I learned that the journey most of us would like to take in life wouldn't come when we wanted it to come. It would come in God's timing, which we would then realize was our own timing.

Chapter One
My Journey

I'm the youngest child of six, each of my siblings are five or more years older than I am. My mother had me in her early thirties and my oldest sister was the only girl until I became a part of the family. Needless to say, she wasn't thrilled to know that she was no longer the only girl. To this day we laugh about how she was so upset, however, she had no choice but to love me.

I was raised with four bothers and one sister, I was the last of the Brady Bunch. My siblings all have the same dad, I was the only child with a different father. Life for me became a little lonely and a lot confusing. Most of the time, I felt as if I was fatherless. There was definitely a father-daughter void, not only in my life, but also in my heart. I really don't know what happened to my mom and my dad's relationship, but from my understanding, my mom was married but separated from her husband when she and my dad began dating. From that union, I came about.

Growing up, I was surrounded by friends who had their mother and father in the home. I always desired that living situation, but it wasn't in the plans for me. I was destined to be in a one parent household. What hurt me the most about not having my dad there was that once he moved on with his life, he got married and became stepdad to his wife's son. It was hard for a young girl to understand why her father would take care of another man's child without taking care of his own child as well. The hurt for me was real and it shined even more light on the void I felt at being my dad's only daughter and not having him in my life.

To make matters worse, my step mother never really cared for me or my other siblings because we weren't her biological children. Her feelings toward us brought about a lot of negative energy in me because it made me feel as if her only concern was her own household. Any children my dad may have had before she became a part of his life didn't seem to matter to her.

I also understood that my dad lived in another state, but I still felt that even though I lived far away from him, I could have still been called by my father and she, my stepmother, could have shown interest in me as well. The only time I would talk with my dad was if I called him, so I stopped trying to reach out to him and let the whole situation go. If he wasn't going to call me, I definitely wasn't going to call him.

Once I got older and had my kids of my own, my dad became ill. That's when he began to play the part of grandad to my kids. He had changed, but it still seemed to me as if nothing had changed with his wife. When she and I did talk, she told me that she felt as if we only called him when something was needed, and she felt that we should call him more often. I found that her thoughts about the situation were a little hard for me to swallow because when he wasn't sick, when he was perfectly well and able, him having contact with us didn't seem to matter at all.

When I was younger, I used to imagine my mother and father being under the same roof together, loving me and caring for me. I would see my elementary friends with their parents and siblings and I just knew that what I saw happening with them, was how life was supposed to be for me as well. I imagined it to be me in the home with a complete family. Yet, my reality didn't match my imagination no matter how much I wished it.

Our house was a one parent household with my mom working to take care her kids and no adult male figure. My siblings' father visited them and picked them up, but I would be left at home because their father was not my father. Why he didn't take me with them, I can't really say, but him not taking me with them made me feel fatherless and lonely.

Some weekends I felt extremely lonely and wanted my father who was then living in Alabama. I always felt that even with him being all those miles away, showing interest in me as a father would have made a big difference in my life. Due to his lack of attention, I had to find a surrogate dad, but that wasn't as hard as I thought it would be.

The closest male there was to be a father to me was my oldest brother. He was a figure that I could trust and follow. I was on his hip and by his side everywhere he went. I was treated like his daughter, he provided for me and took care of my needs. Like a father, my brother set rules that I had to follow. I may not have liked it, but he kept me grounded. He was a nagging man, always trying to get us to do right, but that was because he wanted the best for us. He passed away when I was in high school, but to this day I often wonder how life would have been for me if he was still alive.

My brother was a strict parent, not just to me, but to all our other siblings. He helped our mom raise us by stepping in and filling the position of a father figure in our home. Because he was my brother, I accepted him as a replacement for what I was lacking, but I still missed my father. However, even me having a father figure didn't last very long.

My brother was supportive and protective of me until he passed away in September of 1992 after being diagnosed with HIV. It was my first year of high school when he died of heart failure. Finding my brother lying lifeless on the living room couch was devastating for me. I remember it like it was yesterday.

It was a wet and rainy day as I made my way home from school my ninth-grade year. I came home and walked into the house only to find my three nieces and two nephews sitting on the floor watching television. My brother was sitting on the couch. I proceeded to talk with him because his eyes were open, but he was not responding to me. I looked at him again, very closely, and saw that he wasn't moving at all. I knew something was not right.

I waved my hand across his face, still he did not move or say anything. My heart began to race. I asked my nephew if my brother had said anything while he was on the couch. My nephew told me that he'd asked for a glass of water, however, the glass of water had not been touched. That made my heart beat harder.

Suddenly, I reached out and grabbed his leg, and then I lifted it to see if he would move. He didn't. I went into another room where my step-father, my brother's dad, was and told him that I thought Bernard was dead. He immediately went to my brother's side, called his name twice, lifted his leg as I had done, and walked back into the other room.

My nephew and I didn't say anything to the other kids, we just went outside. I was in a state of shock, I didn't know what to do at the time. I phoned my other brother but got no answer. Because my mom, my sister, and the brother I had just called all worked together, they were already on their way home from work. It was at that moment, right after I'd made the call that they pulled up. That's when I told them what I had just discovered. Everyone was shocked, tears were rolling, but no one really reacted.

It wasn't until the coroner came to pick him up that it hit me. He was really gone. The only father figure that I'd had was gone and he was never coming back. My sister and I cried like crazy on that cloudy day. We immediately felt the void my brother left behind. Not only did he touch our lives, he touched a lot of people including our other family members. He was loving, caring, and would give you the shirt off of his back if he had to or if you asked him for it. Now he was no longer there to give anyone anything anymore.

Later on, we found out the cause of his death. It wasn't the HIV that took him away, it was heart failure as a result of the HIV that did it. When my brother passed, my world was left in shambles. As I grew older, his teachings, leadership, and parenting affected my life in such a positive way that it made me eventually appreciate his rules. But it would be a long while before I finally got to that place of appreciation.

Chapter Two
The Adult Life

For my mother, the passing of our brother, her son, was devasting too, yet she never expressed any sorrowful emotions. Everyone thought it was because she was being strong for the family; I do believe that to be true. But one night my mom was in the living room listening to my brothers' collection of records as she often did, when she suddenly began to scream out loud.

"God, why did you take him so soon? I need him!"

Instantly, I got out of bed and ran to the room she was in only to find her on her knees crying. Her pain was so heartbreaking that it brought me back to my own pain, back to the memories of my brothers' passing all over again. And that pain made me deal with the undeniable realization that he had really left us. The rock of our family was gone, and he'd been taken from us too soon.

I was not only too young to have to deal with the loss of a brother, I was also too young to deal with the loss of another father. My dad had abandoned me in life, my brother had gone away from me in death. Life for me had changed dramatically.

Without my brother there to look after me, I no longer had any guidance; I was running the streets, doing what I wanted to do. I had changed, not for the good but for the worse. I began to hang out with brothers and cousins, all of whom were, again, much older than me. I guess, in a way, I was still looking for someone older to be there for me. But that's not exactly what happened.

Instead of being led and guided by my older family members, I was being influenced by them, and not in a good way. Everything they did, I did it as well, but because I was younger, when I did it, it was illegal.

At the age of fifteen, I was living like an adult. I was clubbing, using fake identification, doing any and everything I wanted and there was no one around to stop me. I was only able to get away with those behaviors because my mom was a working mom raising six kids. She was always gone, so, I did it all without any fear of being caught. I don't fault my mother in any way because she did what she had to do to take care of six kids. And she did a good job of it. However, her having to work all of the time left me unsupervised and open to the troubles the world had to offer me.

People around me would say that I had it good because of the freedom I possessed, but what they didn't understand was that I wanted a different life. I didn't want freedom to do whatever I chose, I wanted the life my friends had, a life that gave me a home with a mother *and* a father. I wanted a life like the other young girls I knew.

Although I was a teenager in age, that freedom people envied me having left me as an adult in my mind and in my actions. There was no one there to lead me and direct me. I was guided by my own decisions while most other girls my age were guided by their parents. However, God, in His loving care for me, kept me covered even as I lived life on my own terms. I just didn't know He was looking out for me back then.

I did attempt to do the things kids my age were doing, but that stuff wasn't fun for me. I tried being a cheerleader, but that didn't work because I didn't have the same kind of support as the other girls. Seeing their parents there with them, supporting what they were doing, and knowing that I didn't have my parents around made me feel out of place. It felt like no one cared and like I was depending on someone else's mom to support me.

Cheerleading was something I wanted to do, not just for their attention, but it was also to give them a reason to be proud of me. However, how could they be proud of me if they never showed up and therefore had no clue what I was involved in?

Then there was the fact that I was not the most popular kid in school. I'd tried to fit in, but when that didn't happen for me, when I realized that I just didn't belong, I turned to a life of the streets. I never seemed to have a problem fitting in there. I didn't blame any of the adults in my life for the direction my life had taken, but I do remember telling myself that when I had my own kids, I would always be their number one supporter no matter what. I didn't want them to feel the way I felt. Alone. To this day, I've stuck to my word.

Over time, as I got older, I finally began to understand why my mom wasn't there and I wasn't as angry or as bothered by their lack of support anymore. Being a teenager that was living life as an adult was exciting because I was able to do things my friends couldn't. Yet, when I became an adult, drinking and going to the club was no longer interesting. I had already done all of it, illegally. Was I proud of it? No. But that was the way my life had been setup.

While my friends were preparing for high school graduation and college, while they were ready to get out into the world and make things happen, I was just trying to figure out how to live my life. I followed suit and went to college like they did, but unlike them, I had something extra. That freedom I had that they all envied got me in a predicament where I'd already had my first child. A daughter.

What a lot of people had no clue about was the fact that throughout my childhood years, I'd experienced sexual intercourse. Not because that was something I'd wanted to do, and it wasn't even at own my will, that had happened at the will of someone else. I'd been molested at an early age, something I'd never shared with others because of the shame I'd felt about it happening to me at all.

I felt ashamed and alone and I was tired of going through things. And still, even after having a father that ignored me and wasn't there to protect me or stop me from being molested, after losing the only father figure I had in my life, and after having family members that weren't there to support me in the positive things I'd tried to do, life continued to throw me curve after curve.

I was seventeen and just finishing high school when I met and became pregnant by my daughter's father. We weren't in a relationship because he was already in one with the mother of his first child, a woman I didn't know existed until I was six-months into my pregnancy. Instead of staying with me, and to save what was left of the relationship with his child's mother, he denied my daughter, which turned out to do even more damage than the lies he'd first told in our relationship. Things just seemed to keep getting worse.

During the last trimester of my pregnancy, my daughter's father was carted off to prison. Even while incarcerated, we argued a lot. Soon, we stopped talking to each other altogether. I was left completely alone, and his family wouldn't help me because he had denied that my daughter was his child. I only had my mother and sister to help me raise my baby. Although they weren't happy at the fact that I had a child while I was still a child myself, they refused to let me go at it alone.

I still went to college after having my daughter; I wasn't going to let the difficulty of being a single parent and a college student at the same time stop me from at least trying to go higher with my education. But it didn't take long for me to begin to feel as if school just wasn't for me. However, add to everything that was already going on the fact that I was trying to attend private schools which cost me sixty-thousand dollars in loan debt, and you had the perfect storm of events that made me want to quit school altogether.

And things just kept getting worse. After everything I'd done to get into college, to stay in college, and to pay for college, I only obtained enough credits for an Associate degree and that was after going to three or four different schools. I had no clear direction for my life, I was just existing with no clue of what to do or of how to do it. It was at that point that I just gave up on school.

Even with getting an education, I still had no clue what I was supposed to be doing in life. I existed by doing whatever without God's consent, and while not healing. But instead of putting all the pain and hurt from my childhood on the back burner of my mind, I just moved on through my life the best way I knew how while carrying the load of hurt and pain right on top of my chest.

Chapter Three
Divorce Wasn't in the Plan

I'm now a single mother of three, but that wasn't how I saw my life going. I had better plans for myself, plans that still included my children, but under much different circumstances. My plans were that I would still be a mother, but that I would be a happily married mother of three. However, no matter how I thought things would go for me, no matter how much I tried to direct things one way, my life always seemed to be on a path of its own. A path that always seemed to sucker punch me or blindside me. Like when it came to my marriage.

I had been married for twelve years and eleven months. Two weeks before my husband and I should have been celebrating our thirteen year wedding anniversary, two weeks shy of my thirty-ninth birthday, the man I thought was the only man for me became the man I was about to divorce. Although there had been bumps and bruises throughout the marriage, I never expected it to come to an end. But it did.

The year 2017 taught me a lot as it broke me down as well.

Leading up to that year, my husband and I were struggling to keep our marriage together. I started seeing another side of the man I thought I'd spend forever with, a side I had never seen before. I felt as if God was telling me that my marriage was over.

My husband reached a point where he said a lot of things that hurt me. In fact, it got to the point where we both started saying things that hurt each other. Hurt people hurt people. If I never believed those words before, I believe and understand them now.

Something deep in me told me that he had been seeing someone else, which, of course, he denied. I asked him often if he was seeing another woman and the more I asked him, the more he lied. The more he lied, the more the feeling grew that he was being unfaithful. I finally got the revelation of his lies, but it didn't come from him, it came from the girl he'd been seeing.

My husband's mistress called me, and when she did, she not only told me a lot about their relationship, she also told me all the things he'd told her about me. I was devastated and even more so because I didn't get that truth from him. To this very day, I still haven't gotten the truth about the dissolution of our marriage from the man that had once vowed to be true to me.

When you are fighting for something, it takes two, you can never fight alone. I was fighting for our marriage, my husband was not. In fact, he stopped fighting the day he started seeing someone else while married to me. I began to say, "God I get it." That's when I began to surround myself with spiritual people. I sought counseling and started changing the thoughts I had toward myself.

In March of that year, I filed for divorce, which was a surprisingly smooth process. I thought I would cry when it was over, but I didn't. I believe it was God letting me know that I had made the right decision. Some people celebrate divorces, but not me, I'll never celebrate when a covenant has been broken. All I could say was farewell and I wished him good luck.

A divorce is a lot like a funeral. The separation of the spouses is there, just as you are separated from one who dies. The emotions slowly die, the hopes and dreams are eventually buried, never to come to fruition. And the life you once lived has abruptly become a thing of the past. The only difference between divorce and a funeral is that the bodies of the wife and the husband are still present on earth. Both alive, just no longer together. That's how I felt while going through my divorce.

During the process, I was confused about life. I was mad, disgusted, and frustrated with myself because I'd tried to do everything right and nothing was going right for me. I tried church as a way to cope with what I was dealing with, but that didn't last long.

I felt that the church had let me down on several occasions. From my wedding day being held up because of fifty dollars owed to the musician, to people treating me like I was nothing, the church had not proven a safe and secure place for me. So, I developed an attitude that kept me away from church. I came to truly believe that I didn't have to go to church because God knew my heart. At that point, I was really lost.

Even though I may not have needed the actual church building, I did need a connection with God. The disconnect from God was the exact reason I couldn't find peace or a place of comfort. I was disengaged from the one Man I really needed. I was at a place where I had not only severed my connection with

God, I also did not depend on Him anymore. Because the moment I'd decided that I didn't need church anymore, I'd also let go of all things pertaining to church.

I no longer prayed like I used to, in fact, I found myself only praying when I needed Him. I had become a conditional prayer, meaning that I only prayed when the conditions in my life placed me in need of Gods help. I'd lost any real connection with our Savior.

I was jumping from church to church trying to fit in. I was looking for a church home and nothing was there for me. But contrary to what I had been thinking, the church wasn't my problem. In reality, the church had never been my problem. Me and my expectations of people was my problem.

I needed to get to a place in life where I stopped looking for acceptance from people, I needed to understand that the only acceptance I needed was from God. It took me almost a lifetime before I figured that out and when I did figure it out, I was fighting yet another battle in my life, a battle with my ex-husband.

He and I weren't getting along. No matter what I said or did, according to him, nothing was ever right. To make matters harder, my kids were suffering as well. They were dealing with the fact that things never seemed change for the better for us, they always seemed to get worse. With the separation of me and their father, with me being out of work and on sick leave, funds became low and it wasn't long before we were facing eviction. No one knew what I was going through except for a select few people. I was too ashamed to speak on what I was facing because in my mind I was supposed to have it all together. I didn't.

Not having a clue what I was going to do with three kids, one of them in college, and an eviction looming, I had to figure out a way keep a roof over our heads. And I had to do it as soon as possible. Things were not looking good at all. To top it all off, while going through the divorce and dealing with the threat of eviction, I received a phone call on July 3rd telling me that my father had passed away. Three weeks after that, on July 25th, my aunt passed away.

Things weren't looking good for me either because I'd had an incorrect diagnosis as it pertained to my eyesight. Had I not gotten the correct diagnosis when I did, and had I not taken that correct diagnosis seriously, I probably wouldn't be able to see at all right now. I was losing my dignity, I was losing who I was, and I felt as if I was being forced to accept things that I shouldn't have had to accept.

People started looking at me as if I done so much wrong, but they never understood my pain because it wasn't their pain. However, I pushed, prayed until something happened. I fought, I cried, and I pled for sanity, and still, everything continued going on a downward spiral. One of the things that added to my distress was how I was handling it all. I would focus on my circumstances and my situations and on how big they were. I never focused on God and how big He was. And that was my problem.

In the midst of all of those storms, I had to find the faith to realize that God was still God. I had to somehow understand that He always finds a way to show us that He is still, and always will be God. I had to muster up strength in God that I didn't know I had and I had to do it quickly because a lot was happening that was keeping me in a constant state of distress and worriment.

People speak on faith a lot, but do they really have faith? Faith comes from within, it's a deep trust that we have with our Father. Oftentimes, we don't have enough faith, so when we face certain situations, we want what we want to happen right then and there. We don't want to allow God the time to perfect whatever it is that we want and to give it to us at a later date if He decides to give it to us at all. Well, I found out the hard way that God's timing and His decisions are always best.

My faith is now stronger than it has ever been, but I had to stand still and let God work to realize that. I had to *not* question God's work and just allow Him to work on His timing. I had to learn that everything would work itself out. If you don't believe me, try having a little faith and see how our Father moves on your behalf.

Chapter Four
Through The Storm

Going through the pain, being deceived, talked about, and criticized, I felt like I was losing everything. Not knowing what to do or how to do it became overwhelming for me. Things were so intense that I even went far as trying to end my own life. But who would I really have hurt had I succeeded at doing that? Myself by destroying my life, and my kids by removing their mother from them.

Just as I had suffered a void in my life without my father, my children would have suffered a void without their mother. And the thing that would have made their loss that much more unbearable was the fact that their mother would have given up her life over a man that continued to live his life regardless.

After that realization set in, my first thought was to go back to Atlanta to live with my mom. I knew everything would be easier that way. However, I decided against that, I didn't want to keep running from my problems. It was time I started facing them head on. I was clueless on how I was going to stomach what I was going through, but it had to be done.

I was without a husband and was living as a single parent. I was surrounded by people I thought had my best interest at heart, but they had turned their backs on me. There was no way I could continue living like that. The stress was so overwhelming that crying was all I did. That's when I began to realize that I was loving man more than I loved God.

I understood that God is a jealous God and that no one should come before Him or be put before Him. I had been doing things all wrong, I had been putting the people before God and not putting God before the people. And the consequences of doing that had taken its toll on me.

At that point, I understood that all I could do was depend on God because man continued to let me down. It was time to put God before the people. I knew I didn't deserve what I was going through and I knew there were better days ahead, but what I didn't know was how I was going to get to those better days fast. Well, guess what? I did get to those better days and it didn't happen fast. It all happened in God's timing.

Honestly, I still have issues dealing with my hurt. I'm still working on some things that God knows I haven't let go of, but it's coming. A day when the hurts and pain is no longer there is coming, I believe that. I don't believe I've completely forgiven those that hurt me, and I know that's where the struggle comes from. But with time and with God, all those things will have passed, and I will have grown on to something else. I still have to accept that people will let us down, but God will not. Once I get that rooted in me, I know I'll be okay.

When people say no, God can always say yes, I am a living

testimony of that. I was in so many situations where I was told no by people and God showed up and showed me that He is God and that I should depend on Him. I was in situations where I was forced to make decisions that I didn't want to make, but I knew the time had come where I could no longer delay in deciding. I had no other choice. I was forced out of situations that I didn't want to leave and could not understand why. But at the end of it all, I had to trust the process, hold on to faith, and push forward knowing that God was working it out for my good.

I had to stop choosing sadness and bitterness and anger and unforgiveness and learn to choose happiness. However, happiness was something that I hadn't felt in so long that I wasn't even sure what it was or how to choose it. I was accustomed to what I thought was happiness, but in reality, what I had experienced was nowhere near what happiness was supposed to be.

I didn't want to trust what was ahead of me. I had grown so comfortable dwelling on the past, whether it was good or bad, that I was struggling with focusing on the future. The past was all I knew, and as uncomfortable as my past was, I was familiar with it. I knew it like I knew the back of my hand, thus I was more comfortable dwelling on it than I was focusing on a future that was to come. The past I knew, I trusted what I knew even if I didn't like it. The future was a mystery to me and I was very uncomfortable with the unknown.

I knew that I had to have faith. I had to let go of it all and give it to God because He will direct your path while you continue the journey not worrying about your past. It wouldn't be easy, but the only way I was going to know what was best was by letting God guide me. I had to be willing to go through the process in order to get through the storm.

In your own life, do not blame man for your situation, you have to take responsibility yourself. Never dwell on the mistakes you have made because the mistakes of your past make you better for what's ahead of you. Through my process, I had to learn it all the hard way, but never will I once say that I regret what I've been through.

Through my storm I used to point the finger at anyone and everyone, but while pointing one finger at others, there was always three fingers pointing right back at me. I came to understand that growth came by acknowledging my faults in a situation and allowing God to work on me instead of blaming others. It was a hard process.

On my journey, I also came to realize that God always has the last say. His say may not be what you want, but it's for sure the word you need in order to run this race called life. When you think you have it all, you will always be disappointed. Why? Because you can never have it all when God is not involved.

What is given to you can be taken away when you love people and things more than you love your Creator. God created us all as equals, but He knew our lives would not be the same. Your purpose will not be my purpose. His plan for your life will not be the plan He has for my life. So, stop worrying about others, live for God, and everything He promised, He will uphold.

In the book of Deuteronomy chapter 31 and verse 6, it reads, *'Be strong and courageous. Do not be afraid or terrified because of them, for the LORD your God goes with you; he will never leave you nor forsake you.'* God has you even when you're at your weakest point, when you don't know which way to turn. He is there through the darkest hours and He for sure is there when the sun is shining. All you have to do is have faith.

Your tears will never go unnoticed just as your prayers will never go unheard. When you don't think He is there, know that He is our God, He won't leave you or forsake you. Know that this too shall pass and that your darkest days will soon become your brightest days. Just trust and believe.

Chapter Five
Understanding Gods Love

I was looking for that happy place and had no clue where that happy place even began. Because I had gone through so much in life, I contemplated what caused those complications, hoping it would reveal not only what had gone wrong, but what I could have done right. In that process, I realized that all of my problems came from loving the wrong people and from not feeling as if I was loved in return. I decided that since my sadness and hurt came from an abundance of neglect, my happy place had to have been in something that I didn't have an abundance of. So, I tried looking for what I had been missing all along.

All of my life I had been missing love from a man. But not just love from any man, love from a good man. I had been loving man more than I loved me, and I had been loving them so hard that it often slipped by me that I wasn't being loved by them in return. I just wanted to be loved, but the love I was searching for was real love and it was the kind of love that man could not give me no matter how hard they may have tried. At that point in my life I thought that loving a man was all I needed. Then I began realizing that I had to love God first, and then man, *a good man* that was filled with God, would appear to fulfill my desires.

When you're young and you don't take things into consideration, when you don't take life seriously because you're wrapped up in society and in how good the devil makes things seem to you, love will always come to you. However, it will come to you the wrong way. It will come to you suddenly and from the wrong direction because you're in such a rush to have it and everything else immediately. But slow down and take your time, good things always come to those who wait on God.

Understand that waiting never hurt anyone, especially when you're waiting on God. When you rely on Him, you will find that in the waiting is preparation for things to come in your life, and that somehow He is setting you up for something great somewhere down the line. Patience is a virtue. Waiting without complaining can be difficult, but when you trust and have faith in God, why complain about what you are waiting for? Just know that when it's your time, it's your time. No matter what it may seem like or look like, it will all be worth the wait.

Although I know this now, I didn't know it then, so I didn't wait on anything. In fact, I practically rushed into everything. My childhood hadn't been filled with someone telling me what I needed to expect from a man or what I should've expected from God. Being molested at an early age and not knowing what love really meant left me with no understanding of what it meant for someone to really love me and how love should really feel.

As time went on, my desire to be loved grew and grew until I was almost desperate to feel as if someone loved me. I wanted love and I wanted it right then and there. I didn't want to wait for it anymore. I was still trying to do things my own way, in my own timing without consulting God and without allowing Him to lead me.

My hurt, anger, and misunderstanding had me looking for a man to love me like *I* wanted him to love me. However, I had no clue what it really meant to love someone or what it really meant to be loved. So, as clueless as I was, I rushed into the journey of looking for love and it lead me to being married and divorced with still no understanding of the true meaning of love.

It was time for me to stop doing things my own way and get a personal relationship with God. And I needed to do that, not only for the salvation of my soul, but also so that I could understand the real meaning of what it was I had been searching so hard for. Love.

Chapter Six
Pay Attention

When I first started writing this book, I wrote a step-by-step journey of my life. I chronicled what happened from childhood to my adult life until one day I started thinking that what I was writing was boring. I convinced myself that no one wanted to hear a drawn-out story about someone's boring life. So, I stopped writing and thought more about what I was doing.

While thinking, I realized that I did want to tell my life story, but I also wanted my book to have meaning. I wanted there to be purpose in sharing my story. I desired to help others overcome what they had lost in the midst of their journey, and I knew that the only way I could do that was by sharing the harsh reality of my own life travels.

One thing that helped carry me through my journey was coming to the realization that not every bad thing that happened in my life was the devil's work. God has His way of working to get your undivided attention. Some things in your life are allowed to happen to open your eyes, to help you see what God is trying to get you to see. He allowed me to go through a lot so that I could see His purpose and His plan for me. We as people become so blind to how God works that we believe everything bad is nothing but the devil's work. But God shows up in every form and fashion to get His people's attention. I went through life not knowing the difference.

Another reason I was unable to see what God had in mind for me was because I didn't really take church seriously. I played church. I grew up in church thinking I had it all together because I went to church. But I never understood His purpose nor His plan for my life. I did what Grandma raised me to do, and that was to go to church, but I never met God while I was there. Now, here I am, thirty-nine years old, still trying to balance my life and still trying to figure out what is God's purpose and plan for my life. Had I paid attention, I would probably have a better understanding today.

Back then I didn't pay attention, though. I was in church for every occasion, Sunday school, bible study, spring break camp, summer camp, I was even part of the choir and couldn't sing a bit. You name it, I did it, because that was my background, that was my upbringing. As a result, you would think I had some knowledge of what God wanted for me and for my life. I didn't have a clue, because I didn't pay attention. I'm just now figuring out that all I had gone through was to lead me to His purpose and His promise for my life.

The Bible says in Proverbs 22:6, *'Train up a child in the way he should go; even when he is old he will not depart'*. So, I was doing what I had been trained to do. By going to church, I never thought that I had turned away from God. I thought I knew God. I could even quote my favorite scripture from the Bible. But the real question was whether or not I really knew God. The answer to that question was simple. I did not know Him.

I didn't know God and I didn't trust His process. I knew that if I prayed to Him, some things would happen in my favor, but as soon as things didn't happen in my favor, it wasn't God that caused the problem, it was nothing but the devil. Through my process, I would have understood what was going on if I really knew who God was. I would have known that God also can tell you no in the process of your journey and not grant your every request.

While looking for the Love of God, I learned that I had to understand God's promise in order to understand His purpose and plan for my life. I had to come to the realization that God's love can take you to eternal life; man's love won't and can't do that. In fact, the love of man won't take you very far. It can, and a lot of times will, lead you to hurt, pain, depression, and disgust. The only way to recover from that is to get back to the love of God.

We can try to avoid Him and we can say we're not ready for Him, but we need Him in every situation and in every circumstance. The first person we're supposed to call on when in the midst of desperate times is God, and we should call Him to pull us out of whatever we're in or may be in. We have to stop being conditional prayers and make prayer part of our everyday routine. Don't just call Him because of your situation, call Him in the midst of your everyday life.

Chapter Seven
Looking for Love in Man

As I continued to play church heading into my adult life, I made a lot of wrong turns. Life, I learned, is like a map. God has our life all mapped out for us, but in order to learn the purpose of the life He gave us, we have to understand the plan, His plan. Along the way there will be bumps and bruises because no one's life is perfect, but if we trust Him, we can make it through anything.

We have a way of ignoring God and doing things our way first, but that only works until it all goes wrong. Then we want to know Gods way and what He has to say about things. I made a lot of wrong turns on the map of life because I'd taken the hurts I'd experienced and used them the wrong way.

As I've said before, growing up as a child, my father wasn't in my life. The disconnection from him didn't allow me to experience the love between a father and a daughter. That's why I struggled with the love between *the* Father and me, His daughter. Regardless of that, my dad was still a man that I loved and that everyone else love so dearly.

The father-daughter bond is something that a man should always give his daughter. Why? Because he's the first man she will ever love, and the love he shows her will teach her how a man should treat a woman. People may think differently, but I learned this as I was growing up and it made a big difference in my life. Not having that bond made me really crave love from a man, so I looked for it all by myself. I had a plan, I was going to be someone's wife. My kids were going to grow up in a house with love from me and their father. And we were going to have the perfect little family. It was set in stone.

Looking for love, I became pregnant with my first child right out of high school. However, love wasn't part of that relationship. Even though I gave birth to a daughter, Kamitra, part of me was still missing because her father had other plans that didn't include us. So, I had to continue my journey alone.

My daughter was six months old when I met the next man I would get into a relationship with. I had no clue that seven years later I would be married to him and that I would love him dearly. I was young, but I just knew God had answered my prayers for a permanent and perfect family by sending him into my life.

In the midst of this love journey that I was on, a storm rolled my way. I became pregnant with my second child, a child that I did not carry to full term. I had a miscarriage. The pain came suddenly and unexpectedly. I was hurting and I couldn't understand why. The pain was bad enough that it caused me to go to the hospital. I was really stressed, but the nurse told me not to worry and that whatever the outcome, it was all part of God's plan. I lost the baby and that same nurse told me that I would have another baby in God's timing.

I became pregnant two more times and suffered two more miscarriages. I was disappointed, hurt, and upset, trying to figure out why that was happening to me. Mind you, I wasn't married, but I was with the man who would later become my husband. During that time, he hadn't been doing things the right way, but I ignored the signs. I chose to stick it out and I figured that my desire to stay pretty much summed up my answer of what God's plan was for my life. I ended up once again pregnant, this time with my daughter Destiny. Because it was a high-risk pregnancy, I was on strict bed rest. It was a tough forty weeks.

After I birthed Destiny, I was told that she would be my last child because I couldn't have any more kids. Two years later, I was pregnant and very confused. I just knew that this pregnancy wasn't going to last because the doctor said no. However, the doctor was wrong because God said yes. I gave birth to my last child, my precious boy, Wayne.

That particular pregnancy almost brought us to death, but eventually we both made it through alright. With two more beautiful kids, another girl and a boy, my family was complete. I now had three kids and a husband. At that point, I thought that I had it all because I was living out my dream of being a wife and a mother. As it turned out, God had other plans for my life, and I didn't understand anything that was taking place.

Through it all, I hadn't been waiting on God; I'd made every decision and took every action myself. Eventually, because it wasn't God's plans I was living out, things were destined to fall apart somewhere down the line. I'd seen all kind of signs, but I wanted what I wanted when I wanted it, so I ignored those signs and kept doing what I wanted to do. I did not want what God had for my life, so my map of life started to take some twists and turns that I definitely was not prepared for. Why? Because I hadn't put God first. In fact, I hadn't included God at all. I was focused on my husband and my kids both first and last. But I quickly learned that when God is not in your plans, no matter what those plans are, they will not succeed.

Not understanding the real meaning of love caused me a lot of unnecessary problems. Anytime a man gave me the attention I wanted and thought I needed, I was happy because that attention was love to me. But everything that looks and sounds good isn't necessarily good. And you become confused trying to understand how what you just knew was good put you in such a bad place.

Because I had been looking for the wrong kind of love, life started throwing me curve after curve. Had I just paid attention when I was going to church, had church not been just something I was trained to do, I would have understood His word and my situation would have been a lot different. But trust me when I say there are no regrets that were the process I had to take to get me where I am today. And it was the journey I needed to take to get me where I'll be in the future.

The Bible quotes in Proverbs 18:22, *He who finds a wife finds a good thing.*' Not once did it say for a woman to find a man. But I decided to make my own verse and find my own man, a man I thought would be perfect for me. I'd made a huge mistake when I decided to seek my own understanding and not God understanding. Doing things my way, I became married after seven years of being in a relationship, and I remained married for twelve years and eleven months before I finally became divorced.

You might say that was a long marriage, and by today's standards it could be considered that. However, by Biblical standards it wasn't long at all because according to the vows we took; it was supposed to last a lifetime. It was supposed to last until death did us part. If I hadn't been so focused on being loved, I would have paid attention to all of those signs in the beginning. I would have seen that the answers were right front of me and not continued that journey. But I dismissed those signs and remained on the journey because I felt that I loved that man more than I loved life itself.

In addition to everything else that I'd been dealing with, I felt as if I didn't get the proper chance in my marriage that I should have gotten before it became a disaster. Again, it was God showing me that I should let go. I didn't listen. I was still fighting to stay married, but it didn't take long for me to realize that I was fighting alone. One thing is for certain, you can't fight to save anything by yourself. It takes two.

When you don't know the love of God, you'll never understand how another human being can love you. My lack of understanding had me divorced and raising three kids on my own. Throughout the battle my husband and I were going through, neither of us wanted to listen to the other, so nothing worked for either of us. The kids were stuck in the middle of a disintegrating family because of choices that were made for their life. I was hurt, but I don't blame the man I chose to live my life with. I blame myself because I didn't have the right plan, I didn't have God's plan.

Never rush out and try to find love on your own, wait on God to send you your Boaz, your true love. Depending on God is the only way you'll know that the love you have is real. Had I waited on God, had I made God a priority in our marriage, maybe things would have been different. But I didn't wait on God, I didn't make

God a priority, and the map of my life took me on a journey of hurt, for me and my kids, that could have been avoided.

In the midst of it all, I learned that you can't live for people, you have to live for God first and that's the only way you'll know what's what. You'll find that God places people in your life for a reason, for a season, or for a lifetime. You have to be wise enough to know the difference. You must know who is in your life, what their purpose is for being a part of your life, and how long their season is in your life. However, the only way you will ever know that is by having a real relationship with God, the One who is control of your life. When you have a relationship with Him, you'll know that He will often give you what you want, but you'll also know that what He gives you is not always there to stay. Everything, the good and the bad, is a part of your process.

While growing closer to God, you have to be careful of what you pray for and of how you pray for it. One thing about our God, He will often give you what you ask Him for, but you won't know what the outcome will be if He is not part of the plan. If it doesn't fit, don't force it. Just like puzzle pieces, if it doesn't fit, you can't make it belong.

God had given me what I wanted. I prayed for it, He gave it to me, but it wasn't part of God's plan. When what He gave me didn't work out to my liking, I was then saying that it was nothing but the devil. In actuality, it was God doing His work and showing me that He is God.

I have always known myself to be a person that loves hard. I believe I loved that way because of my background, because of always wanting to feel loved, always wanting a family with both parents involved. That's why I loved my kids hard; I wanted to give them what I didn't grow up with. However, I went about it all wrong. I took my hurt and pain and used it to look for someone to love me instead of overcoming what I had been through and being a better me. I was desperate to find love instead of letting love find me.

With all that I have endured, my experience with men has made me become a better me, but that's because I decided to give it all to God. I stopped looking for someone and started waiting on that special someone to find me and love me the way God would love me. When real love finds you, you will know. Your heart will beat differently and things will feel so unreal. You just have to trust the process. Don't look for love, let love find you.

Chapter Eight
Acceptance

The process of learning to accept people and things in your life starts with you. I always wanted to be accepted by others no matter the situation. My heart is pure when it comes to others, I love hard in every situation. The love I have for people is very genuine and real because I love to see others happy rather than unhappy.

My love runs so deep, that I'll feel as if I'm drowning, but I'll save someone else's life before I'll try to save my own or even make sure I'm safe. I've never been a selfish person, and never have I behaved selfishly. If I eat, you eat. If I can go above and beyond to put a smile on your face, that's what I'll do.

While living my life as a selfless person, I learned that everyone is not as genuine as you think they are. As a result, it became hard for me to accept people for who they really were. Things with people always changed and seemed to go in different directions. I would feel as if someone was with me and down for me, my heart would be pure toward them, and they were the people I would call my ride or die. At times I would even call them family whether they were blood or not. I thought everyone was like that and really felt that way until situations revealed who they really were.

It seemed that when things got tough, I rode for them, but they didn't ride for me. I was thinking that what was happening couldn't be real. I remember thinking that I'd known this person or those people for so many years, there was no way my friendship with them was coming to an end. But as it turned out, those situations did happen, they were real, and those friendships were coming to an end.

One thing for certain, no matter the amount of years or the time a person is a part of your life, it doesn't mean they are fit for your life. You can meet a person that is genuine and that will ride harder for you within a minute of knowing you than the ones you've known for years. So never let the time you've known a person fool you. I did and it backfired on me.

I'd trusted so many people and faced so many obstacles because of that trust that I began to hold grudges. It was hard for me to accept the betrayals and the abandonments. I questioned myself daily, wondering where I went wrong. Then I began to realize that I didn't really go wrong, I just thought I was loved by others the same way I loved them.

It was during this process I learned that the only acceptance anyone needs in life is to be accepted by God. We don't need to be accepted by earthly people because there's always the chance that they will let us down. There are cold hearted people that couldn't care less about how we feel as long as how we feel doesn't affect them. There are also those that will care about you no matter what and will never let you down. I had been let down and disappointed too many times to count and it was hard for me to trust people anymore, even the good ones.

I'd made some wrong decisions. I'd walked away from friends that had my best interest at heart and I'd put them on the back burner for friends who never had my best interest at heart. Those people were really only there for that season, but because I wasn't as close to God as I should have been, because I had played church for so long, I was confused about who meant me well and who did not.

I soon found that life really is like a box of chocolates and that you never know what you're going to get. There are times you think you've got it all when in reality, whatever it was that you had was all you needed. But at some point you started thinking that what you had wasn't enough. Not appreciating what you have is the fastest way to get caught up. Wanting to fit in and to be accepted by people that are only in your life for a reason, people that you are trying to keep for a lifetime, can only cause you heartache and pain. Everybody isn't for you. If people can't accept you for who you are and for what you are without you having to bring something to the table, those people were never your friends to begin with.

I've been let down by many people. I've seen some of the people I trusted do things to others and treat others a certain way, but never in my mind did I think they would do it to me. I thought I was so different. However, the same games that were being played behind the backs of those who would be hurt, games that were taking place in front of my face, had now been turned toward me. And that was something I couldn't accept.

How was I supposed to accept the fact that people I loved so dearly, people I thought loved me just as I loved them turned, had their backs on me when I needed them most? Their betrayals hurt me to the core, but eventually, the ones that have always been there for me found their way back to me. They returned just in time to lift me up while I knew that I didn't deserve them at all.

Another lesson I learned was to always watch your surroundings because you are no better than the next person. Through my journey, I always wanted people to be pleased with me, so I did anything to earn their approval and their acceptance. It has always been said that actions speak louder than words that was something I lived by. I showed people how I felt about them by the actions I took and not just by the words that came out of my mouth.

People will always remind you of what they did for you, but they struggle with acknowledging the things you do for them. Howbeit, if a person has to say what they did for me, I'm going to question whether what they did for me came from the heart or if they had ulterior motives. Why? Because when things are done from the heart, they will never be thrown in your face. So, when it's all said and done, I'll never once say what I did for anyone. At the end of the day they know exactly what I did and so does God. I don't need to remind anyone of anything.

Giving without receiving is always a blessing from God. This is why you first have to accept who you are within God and then you have to know your worth when it comes to people. Being accepted by others will not happen easily, but when you understand the process and accept who you are, you couldn't care less whether or not others accept you. You'll still give without receiving, knowing that God will eventually bless you in return.

One thing is for certain, you can never please people, so don't even try. Pleasing God gets you where you need to be, and He will direct you in the right direction. He'll show you who you should be connected with, and He'll help you to know why you should be connected with the people you come across. But none of these things can happen if you don't trust Him first and foremost.

Despite any situation you're in, when it comes down to it, your real friends will know exactly who you are and they will accept you for the person you are and not because of what someone else tells them about you. We live in a world of judgment, but my personal philosophy is that you should never judge a book by its cover or let someone tell you about a person. Their perception may not be your perception. The best way to know someone is to get to know them for yourself because every relationship is different.

Chapter Nine
Rejection

Rejection is something I was always afraid of throughout my life. Learning to accept rejection from someone or something is harder for some people than for others. It could be easier for some due to the fact that everyone handles things differently, it could be harder for others for that same reason.

I accepted a lot of things in life because I never wanted to feel rejected by others. I tolerated how people treated me just so that they wouldn't reject me. People would say it was low self-esteem or that I was just say crazy, but a lot of people deal with this on a daily basis and they handle it the same way I did. They try to please everybody with the hopes that no one will reject them.

One thing I have learned in the process is that because everything is in God's timing, being rejected is not as bad as we think. When God says no, He's protecting us from something or keeping us from something or someone that could be harmful to our journey, harmful to His plans for our lives. It is for that reason that we should not become discouraged when it seems as if we are being rejected. Accept what it is and then let it be. I promise, there is something better coming in the process.

Accepting rejection and trusting God sounds easy enough, but I can truly tell you for sure that it's not easy. I went through relationships in my life knowing things weren't right and knowing that I didn't like the feeling of certain things. But because I wanted to be accepted by all, I tolerated things that nobody should have to tolerate just so that I wouldn't have to endure what I struggled with. Rejection from mankind.

When I say I went through relationships, I'm not just speaking of intimate relationships; I'm speaking of all relationships. Friendships, family relationships, work relationships, and spiritual relationships were all a part of my equation. Within my intimate relationships, I found myself agreeing to unbelievable things so that I wouldn't have to face my rejection fear at the hands my significant other. However, when it was all said and done, no matter how good I thought I was in the relationship, the rejection had still been delivered to me on a gold platter.

In any relationship, you have to know your worth. People have a way of misusing you in situations, and the reason why is because they'll prey on you if you don't know who you are and what you deserve. I used the word prey and not pray because that's what it is. Preying is when you hunt someone for the purpose of victimizing them or attacking them. Praying is when you go to God on someone's behalf for the purpose of helping them or uplifting them.

People will sometimes pretend to accept you, all so that they can prey on you. When their true motives are finally revealed, and you see that they never really accepted you, but only pretended to accept you so that they could use you, that form of rejection can hurt more than if they had just rejected you from the very beginning. This world is not easy, neither are the people in it. That's why we have to keep God in alignment; we need Him to help us see through people so that we can know who is for us and who is definitely against us.

The devil will bring his people to you and they will pretend to have a clean heart, knowing all the while that their intentions aren't good. The Bible says in John 10:10, *'The thief cometh not, but that he may steal, kill, and destroy, I came that they may have life and may have it abundantly'*. This scripture means the devil has a plan, but God has a better plan. Just follow Gods path and He will see you through. Know that everything you may think is sent by God is not. Just like I said in my previous chapter, God shows up and shows out, but the Devil shows up as well. You have to learn the difference, and the way you do this is by leaning on Gods understanding and not your own understanding.

Rejection on a job is just like rejection in a relationship. When you apply for a position and are told you aren't qualified, it feels like the world has come to a complete end because it didn't go the way you expected it to go. In our minds, we come up with all the reasons why we didn't get this new position whether we're correct in our thoughts or not.

We'll tell ourselves that the reason another person got the job is because of favoritism, or we'll convince ourselves that those doing the hiring for those positions just don't like us. We'll even go as far as to believe that the hirer knew who was going to get the position and we'll wonder why they even posted the position in the first place.

That was me, I was the person that had said it all and I believed what I'd said to be true to the point that I became angry with the world. What I didn't realize during those times was that the rejection was because there was something better ahead. When man says no, God says, "I have something better".

Life is going to be full of rejection and it's not because you don't fit the part, it's because it was not your timing and it was not meant for your life. Sit back and look at how many times someone said no to you and how you were later blessed with something better. Everyone may have the same hours of the day to succeed in life, but trust and believe, they experienced a lot of rejections in those hours before they got to their success. Don't stress the process. Just trust the timing and look at how both young people and old people become successful within their lifetime.

No matter what kind of relationship it is, it will always take time, effort, and a fair share of rejections before it becomes a success. Marriage, business, promotions, friendship and etc., no matter what it is, just trust the process.

Chapter Ten
Marriage

Marriage is a covenant with God. Time after time I hear people say that marriage is just a piece of paper. I do not agree with that because marriage is so much more than a piece of paper. Marriage is a commitment that you make with your spouse and with your Heavenly Father. I am a believer of God's word. If you feel like marriage is just a piece of paper, you don't know the meaning of that particular covenant and in that case I suggest you seek marriage counseling before you get married and pay close attention during that counseling.

If you choose to go to marriage counseling, you should not get just any marriage counselor, it should be a spiritual marriage counselor. Marriage is a gift from God and it is part of God's plan that men and women should live together as husband and wife. The Bible clearly teaches that the institute of marriage is a covenant between one man and one woman, a lifelong union of two partners created in God's image to govern and manage the earth for Him. Marriage is deeper than people understand, that's why there are so many more divorces than there are people celebrating their union. That sacred institute is not taken seriously anymore.

After being with my ex-husband for so many years, I lost who I was in the midst of it all. During the marriage, I became so complacent with him that I allowed everything to go his way. I didn't think for myself at all and I agreed with him instead of disagreeing when I thought something different. When everything started to fall apart, it was partly because we couldn't see eye to eye anymore. After so many years of me being quiet, it became problematic for him when I finally started to speak out on what I felt was right.

As time went on, things became more and more complicated. He had plans that didn't include me and he didn't take into consideration how our kids would feel when he acted out those plans. He was not only rejecting the marriage, he was also rejecting me as his wife and I thought that was the end of life itself.

Throughout the relationship, we were separated from each other because of issues he had with the law. We got married through it all and of course I didn't know what the outcome of the situation he was facing would be. I decided to plan for what I thought was best, just in case it didn't go the way we would've liked it to go.

When my family made the decision to leave the state of Florida, I decided to move with them. I made that decision because my husband and I were told that he would be away for quite some time. I had only planned to be out of state until everything with my husband was cleared. I had no clue that he would feel as if I didn't think of him when I made that decision.

The thoughts running through my head at that time were about the kids and what was best for them through such a difficult situation. They had already lost their father figure to the system and they were losing their family due to a move to another state. I was thinking about a support system for both them and me. I wasn't excluding my husband, I was preparing us for the worst.

As time went on, we found that he only had to do a year of time which was much better than what we expected. But the communication between us wasn't as clear as it should have been because at one point he agreed with the move, but then I found out that he really disagreed. I hadn't made the decision to be selfish to him, I made the decision because I had three kids and I wanted us to be comfortable.

One thing for certain, I had nothing against anyone. I just felt that me, as a woman, would have been better with the support of my family since the support system of my husband wasn't there. I guess being young, I didn't know that the decision I'd made would lead me to become divorced. After he was released, I tried to make things right, but of course I was the only one trying. He just wasn't as involved anymore.

After making the decision to move back to Miami to be a family with my husband again, I found that his heart was no longer in it anymore. I had set myself up, not knowing what I was about to face. I had to deal with not understanding his anger toward me, with not knowing that the decision I'd made had caused him great hurt. I was also accused of everything he'd been told about me, not things I'd actually done, just things he'd been told. I felt as if I'd never gotten the fair chance to be a wife after he was released.

At that time, I began questioning God's motives, wondering why that was happening to me. I started attending church again, praying for that man like I had never prayed before. I was in need of Gods help. I'd even started quoting the Bible, saying things like, "I know God said that what He put together let no man tear apart." Then I started blaming the devil for what he had done to the marriage.

When nothing worked, I started to accept what I didn't want to accept. My marriage was falling apart and there was nothing I could do about it. As I began to let go and start my life again, I still couldn't seem to find happiness. I began dating, having fun, clubbing, everything and anything to release the pain that had a hold on me. I wasn't seeking God anymore, I was just doing me. Again, I was angry and I felt as if I could do things on my own and be better off. That was a lie.

At some point, I became cordial with my husband and it seemed that things were getting better. That reprieve didn't last. A year later I found myself facing destruction with him and that same foolishness. He still had plans that didn't include me or the kids. It angered me to know that I had fallen for his lies once again, and for an entire year. By this time I was angry and asking God why He continued to do that to me. I was constantly wondering where I was going wrong.

I'd found out that my husband had been telling people everything that had happened in our past. He'd been telling them things that I thought we had moved past. I assumed that maybe all of that was done to get back at me for going to Atlanta and trying to live a normal life. I guess that was his karma against me for not following what he thought I should have done.

I didn't understand what was happening in my life, I was facing suicidal thoughts, and I had no idea what to do. I had been out of work for eight months because once again, I'd put my life in man's hand and not in God's hand. It took time, but I finally learned the moral of that particular story in my life. I was supposed to trust God and trust His process.

You may not know why things are happening to you, but have faith in the reason why God is trying to pull you out of a situation. Maybe we had already grown apart, maybe it wasn't our time anymore and our season had come to an end. We could have made the decision to stay together, but that would have been a decision made without seeking God in the process. As a result of making a decision without God, we could have wound up in the same situation, facing divorce anyway. But this time there would have been more years invested, more feelings invested, and definitely more hurt administered on both parts. Above all, the one thing I learned from all of this is that anything that is God's work won't and can't be tampered with.

This time I did what was best, I filed for the divorce and moved on with life. I held on to my faith, knowing that things would get better for me. I may not have known the road that was ahead of me, but this time around I had to trust God's process. When God's got you, there is no need to look back. Going backwards is a disaster waiting to happen. I didn't understand that until much later.

Today, I don't have a clear understanding of what's about to take place in my life, but I have to have faith and trust the process. It's all about allowing God to lead me. I did a Facebook trivia a couple of days ago and it told me that I should take a break from the thoughts of my past. It said that I had been cheated on and hurt by a trusted someone. It also informed me that I should not keep thinking about it. It said that it was important to let go as well and that I should do just that. Take a break and let go. The trivia results were right.

You don't know how God is going to send His message to you. The day I did the trivia, I was in heavy thoughts about my past and God spoke to me through Facebook. I was shocked because most things I do on Facebook come back with results that aren't true, but this particular day I knew it was God speaking confirmation on what He had already told me. It was my past, so it was time to let go of the hurt and the pain that it brought to me.

When God is working on your life, look at it as a blessing from Him. If your faith is as big as a mustard seed, that's all you need, and God will perform in your life like He never performed before. But you have to have faith, you have to trust God, and you have to trust the process.

The journey I was on didn't only affect me; my kids were affected as well. The energy you feed is not only the energy you will feel, it is also the energy your family, those who love you and care about you, will feel as well. My daughters were hurt, my son never really showed much emotion, but he'd made statements in regard to what took place and how it had affected him. Had I handled the situation better, they probably would have dealt with what was taking place in a much better manner.

No matter how much you try to keep calm in hard situations, you never know how your emotions will go. I am learning that if God had been my source of direction, I would have hurt and I may have been a bit emotional, but I truly believe things would have played out a lot differently. I would have taken a different approach and everybody would have been affected differently, me, my ex-husband, and my kids.

I don't regret anything, I just know that everything worked together to make me a better me. (Romans 8:28) It made me look at things from a different perspective. With time and with God, I found that God has a different plan for those that set out to hurt us. He loves us all even through our flaws, but trust and believe He is not blind to anything we do. Nothing goes unnoticed by him.

To this day, I still do not understand what happened with my marriage, but with the love of God and the faith that I now I have, I don't need to understand what happened. I simply need to thank God for showing up when He did and trust His plan for my life. Even though I didn't want to let go of the marriage, He kept pulling at me until I was forced out.

It is said that if someone is honest and gives you closure after a breakup that could help ease your pain. That may very well be true, but when things or situations are clear to one person and aren't clear to the other person, the person without clarity will never get the closure they may need. Only God can give them that.

Chapter Eleven
Friends

It was very hard for me to be rejected by friends because I didn't have many friends that I was close to on a daily basis to begin with. When I started the relationship with my ex-husband, I dedicated my time to family. I encountered friends in the midst of it all, and there were times that I put in more work for my friends than some of them would put in for me. I'd learned that there's not much you can expect from people, so it wasn't a surprise when they rejected me. However, it does become hurtful when you find that your heart is purer than those you call friends.

I had friends who disconnected from me for their own reasons, and back then I didn't care why. I always felt that I was a true friend and if they left me it was on them. Even as an adult, if I did wrong by someone and they felt a certain way about me, they could have addressed me because that was what I did when I had issues with others. So, if people left me, I felt as if they had opportunity to talk to me, if they chose to leave without doing so, that wasn't my problem. It hurt, but I couldn't take responsibility for their actions.

I have also disconnected with people that I considered friends, and we have reconnected like we never left each other's side. I consider that a lifetime relationship. People have their time in your life, everyone is not intended to stay. Take it with a grain of salt and count it all joy.

There are some people that lean on others to understand the person he or she is dealing with. When that happens, it causes relationships to go wrong because those people never get to understand their acquaintances for who they are. To know me is to love me. When so-call friends walk away without getting to know me for me, they were never fit for the script of my life in the first place.

It has been told to me that where God is taking you, some people can't go on that journey with you. If friends can never really know you and then leave you, they aren't fit for your life. They aren't meant for *the Promised Land* to which God is taking you, and to be honest, they never were.

When you lose people, just know that God will send new people into your life for the connection He needs them to have with you. You may not understand why some were removed from your life at the time, but sometime within your journey you will know exactly why some new people took the places of those that had been removed.

I have had a couple of friends that I have been disconnected from, but because we reconnected and are so close now, you would never think that we had ever been disconnected at all. Because of the true friendship we have, I thank God daily for Shacola, Eboni, and Chunda. They have been through the storm, the rain, and the sunshine of my life and I couldn't ask for anything more. These women supported me, told me when I was right and when I was wrong. Their realness never went unnoticed in my heart and I'm thankful for the support God gave me through them.

There are friends I've met on my own and there are also friends that I consider family that I've encountered through others. They will always have a special place with me. I will forever love Quietta, Ronnie, Antionette, Kierra, and Lisa because they loved me for me. They showed me their true support and they had my back when those I thought should have been there to stand with me did not.

People that know you for who you are, and not based on what others told them about you, will stand with you and stand for you through thick and thin. I went through a lot of hurt depending on others who didn't stand with me through my thick and thin. When people needed me, I was there for them; I support them through any and everything. But when I needed them, they weren't there for me. That's one thing that you have to learn, and you have to learn it fast.

Every heart is not a heart for you. The real person comes out in difficult circumstances, they emerge when it's time to show if they are for you or not. It is in those times that you will find out if they ever loved you for you, or if they were there because you were somehow beneficial to them at the time. During the times of struggle in your life is when you will find out the person's reason or season for being in your life. And sometimes it will hurt you to learn that you were their reason or their season, but never their lifetime.

In the midst of it all, pay attention and by all means learn to read between the lines. The answers are all there. And remember to be careful of who you stand with because when you're in need, the person you're standing with just might be the one that leaves you standing alone.

Later in my life, I met a special friend named Carlos. In the midst of me going through my storm, he was my friend, a confidant with understanding that didn't come with any ill intentions or any ulterior motives. Carlos was just someone I could talk to, someone that would prove to be a good listener. I'm sure at some point I probably got on his nerves talking about everything I was continuously going through, but he never showed me that he was annoyed with me in any way. He was a true supporter.

We became close and through the process of time I learned that he was going through a little storm of his own. It was at that point that we became each other's supporters. As we grew closer, I was wondering why God put this man in my life. Then again, I had been through so many difficult things that I began to wonder if the devil was trying to get me wrapped up in another one of his games. I wasn't sure which reason he was there, but I let the process play itself out.

Over time, Carlos wanted to introduce me to some special people in his life. I was skeptical about meeting them because of our situation, but for him, I did it anyway. It was on an evening that I was sick and had to work the overnight shift that I decided to go with him to meet the friends he was very close to. His friend's face was very familiar to me and I found that the familiarity was due to the fact that his friend and I had attended the same high school. And it turned out that not only did I know Carlos' friend, but I also knew his friend's wife because she and I had gone to high school together as well. I was then re-introduced to Geralda Larkins, the wife of Carlos' friend.

That night she and I talked like we had known each other personally for years. I shared my story with her, she understood, and she opened my eyes to my situation in a way that I had never viewed it before. She explained to me the reason I had to go through what I was going through and even though what she'd said was similar to things I'd heard before, she had a way of putting it that made me get it. The things she'd said sounded so much better coming from a woman of God.

Her words were kind and they lifted my spirit and touched my heart in so many ways on that one night that it was a true blessing being in her presence. She practically spoke life into me. Carlos and I decided then and there that we would attend Soul Harvest Praise Ministry, the church they attended. Since going to their church, I have found that church has become what I had been seeking throughout the storms of my life. I'd needed a connection with God for a long time and I finally got it at Soul Harvest.

Life had thrown me a lot of changes and during the process I didn't have the right connection I'd needed with God. When pastor Larkins and her husband entered my life, I felt as if I was being prepared to start my next chapter. Things began to look differently and I began to understand how to let go through the process of forgiveness. No one is perfect, we all are God's children, and forgiveness is essential for growth.

We must understand that the ups and downs that people bring into our lives are just a part of God's process. Focusing on the hurts caused by some, and remaining in an unforgiving mindset because of it will only hinder our growth. God's timing will never fail you in any situation. Friends will come, and friends will go, but God will always replace them with the people or person that is meant for that part of your life. To accept a friend, you have to first understand how to be a friend. You have to trust God throughout every friendship and you must understand that if it doesn't last, it was time to come to an end. There's an expiration on many items in life, I've come to understand there could also be an expiration on friendships.

Chapter Twelve
In the Midst

I'd reached a place in my life where I'd finally gotten it, I was understanding God and praising Him more and more. However, things started failing me once again, because in the midst of my spiritual growth, that's when the eviction took place.

My funds had become low, and I had been living off of overtime for just about a year and a half. The overtime was a blessing to me because it was very rare that the company I worked for would allow me to work like that. Everything had been going great until the overtime began to slow down and then eventually stopped. I was basically dependent on money that wasn't even guaranteed to me.

Never live your life based on the overtime you work, live within your means, within your base pay rate, because without notice things can change. Times were stressful, but God always made a way to pull me through, to show me that He is still God. Even though I was going through those things, I was still able to stand tall and make decisions that allowed my kids and me to be okay.

I got up every day and did what I had to do to continue living. I believed that regardless of what the outcome would be, things would turn out great. My faith had become stronger, so I knew I would be ok. I stopped stressing and let God do what He said He would do. For one of the first times in my life I was exercising my faith. Not just believing with my feelings but believing with my actions as well. I was scared to fill out applications for apartments because of my past history, but I stepped out on faith and did what needed to be done.

I filled out an application for one particular apartment and was called the next day telling me that I was approved. I moved in three weeks later, but I had absolutely no plans of remaining there. I was trusting God for bigger and better things. My plan was to purchase a home.

Although that one good thing happened, there were still more bad things waiting ahead for me. I received a phone call on July 3rd and the caller informed me that my father had passed away. My father and I had just begun to build our relationship. I always loved him through everything, even though feeling abandoned by him. But I'd never gotten the time to spend with him that I would have loved. All I could say was that at that time we were in a much better place with our relationship than we were when I was growing up.

I didn't take learning that my father had left us easily, but I knew it was God's will. And if I thought my father's passing was hard for me, when I returned to Florida for my father's homegoing, I was told that my aunt, my mom's sister, only had a few weeks to live. That news hit me hard. I began to ask God,

"Why? What is really going on?" But then I paused, reflected on just who God was and said, "God, it's your will. No more pain and suffering for her or my father. So, let them have their wings, they are now in a better place."

It wasn't an easy transition, but I had to trust in God's word. That is what kept me moving forward. The body is borrowed, it is not yours. In 1st Corinthians 6:19 it reads *'Do you know that your bodies are temples of the Holy Spirit, who is in you, whom you have received from God?'* You do not belong to yourself, once your work is done here on earth, He receives you, his angel, home. So, I had to let go and know that I had a couple of angels watching over me. It hurts losing a loved one, but it feels better when you know they are with your Father. Paul said that to be absent from the body is to be present with the Lord. Knowing that is what helped me to move forward, both in life and in God.

Chapter Thirteen
How Did I Get Here?

Somehow, I'd arrived at a place where I felt sad and lonely. I didn't know where to turn or what to do. Like I said previously, God has a timing on your life and only He understands the timing. You will eventually understand if you just be still. Proverbs 3:56 teaches us to, '*Trust in the Lord with all your heart and lean not on your own understanding; in all your ways submit to him, and he will make your paths straight.*' All I could do at that time in my life was trust God.

People were exiting my life like crazy and I was feeling the loss that came with that. I had been lied on. I had been talked about. I had been criticized and cheated on. I was tired and wanted the craziness to end. But what made me different from anyone else out there in the world that had been going through the same things? I knew and trusted that God had better plans ahead for me.

In life, you will never know and you will never really understand why people do the things they do. Sometimes they will never admit where they were wrong and they will have the world looking at you in so many different ways. However, this is not the time to give into defeat, this is when you lift your head up high and never look down. Why? Because the God we serve is never ashamed of us or of who we are.

It was during one of my sad times that I asked Pastor Geralda Larkins, "How do you continue your life for God knowing that you are not completely converted to Gods ways." For example, I was living right, but there was still an area in my life that I was struggling with. Even though I had moved on, had grown past a lot, had started living my life, I was painfully aware that God doesn't condone divorces. In that area I felt as if I had done something seriously wrong and I still needed answers. With all that I had come through, with all that I had gained, I still felt as if happiness was far from me because of this thing.

It was through this process that I realized we will always need God's daily input in our lives. Even when we get to a place where things seem to be going well, we still need Him and He will be there for us if we allow Him to be. God paid our way by being crucified for our sins. Even in the midst of our mistakes, when He knows our hearts and when He knows they are pure, He will still fight on our behalf.

I eventually came to understand that God is not looking for a perfect person, He is looking for a willing person. He is looking for us to know Him and He wants us to know that He knows us. He desires us to love Him and to trust Him and if we know that, in everything we do or think of doing, we will want to consider God and His will. I had to come to this realization before I could understand that God had forgiven me for my divorce even though I had yet to forgive myself. I am now at a place where I am okay with who I am and with the demise of my marriage.

I had to endure a lot of things in my life to get me to where I am today. If had I not had the issues that I'd had, how could I ever be a blessing to others? The truth of that matter is that without my past and without my pains, I would have had nothing to share and no way to bless others with what I'd gained.

Contrary to what I'm sure some will believe, sharing my story was not done simply for me to talk about anyone or to put anyone down. It is for a much deeper purpose than that. The sharing of my story is to help others that are going through similar situations. It is to help those that don't have a clue how to handle their situations or how to adapt to the life God had set up for them from the time they exited their mother's womb.

We are raised in a world where we are taught to plan our own lives. When we do this, God doesn't just sit back and laugh, waiting until we need Him to approve. He's directing and orchestrating from the very beginning, hoping that we will see and live out His plan so that we don't have to hurt unnecessarily when He changes and redirects our lives.

There are plenty of women and men out there that are still lost in this world, still lost in situations they can't overcome. But that's only because they haven't submitted to God yet, or because they have yet to accept Him to submit to Him, or because even though He is always right there, they refuse to see Him.

My story of struggle, acceptance, and finally submission might not be the story for you, but it's for someone. It can help someone who is going through what I have been through to get to where God needs them to be to live out His plan for their life. It's to help them realize that no matter what they have been through, they can always be a blessing to someone else.

Chapter Fourteen
What I Thought I Lost

I thought I'd lost so much in life that some days I would feel like just giving up. I continued to meet people who only cared about themselves. They seemed to never think that their actions could hurt someone else and if they did think it, they seemed to not care as long as the situation benefited them. Then there was the fact that what I thought was for me seemed to never be for me. Even though I wanted it, God would take it away and I couldn't understand why.

There's a meme on the internet that shows a little girl speaking with God. God's hand is extended while He is asking her for her little teddy bear, a bear she is hiding behind her back to keep God from taking from her. She is telling Him how she loves the bear, not realizing that behind His back is a much bigger teddy bear that He desires to give her if she will just let go of the one in her hand. That story is our lives. We want to hold on to what we have because we are so comfortable with it, and we just don't trust God enough to let go of what we have so that He can give us the bigger prize.

That's the mind state I was in when I thought I was losing in so many situations in my life. In reality however, I just didn't trust our God enough to know that He would give me better in every situation. It was during this time that I read somewhere on social media that God will never take away something or someone without the intention of replacing it or them with much better. That was confirmation for my life because the people and things that I had come in contact with left me feeling as if I had lost everything trying to stay connected to them. I didn't realize that they had already played their part in my life and that it was time for God to move me on to my next season.

We will never understand the way God moves in our lives until we get connected to Him. I was confused for years, I even blamed myself for not handling situations differently when in reality, it was handled just like it was supposed to be handled. And it was done that way to open the eyes of my understanding. In order to make it through hard times you have to fully endure your experiences until the bitter end. Yes, it's going to hurt, but the pain is the part that make you a stronger and a better you. I've said this several times, but we *have* to trust the process and have faith in God.

It took me a while to understand what God was doing in my life and that it was Him that was in complete control. I thought I had lost it all when God was just trying to give me something better. I now know that where God is trying to take you, everyone can't go. God will replace unproductive people or negative people in your life with people that will lead you to His promise. Some people that you are with today are not ready for what God is trying to do in your life. So, don't count it as a loss when God removes them, take it as a blessing from our Savior.

I went through it all trying to keep friendships, trying to please people so as not to lose them. But it was never my call for them to stay, that's why things happened the way they did. The fact that I couldn't control those circumstances bothered me for a long time, until I realized that I can love people from a distance.

There's nothing wrong with loving people from afar. It may not seem like you care about them, but it is not that you don't care, it's just that the distance is better for the both of you. It may also be that the person set far away from you may be going in a different direction, doing another assignment for God that is not part of the same assignment God has for you. Take that as a step of favor in your life.

Everyone's assignment is different, and I can't stress enough that we should trust him and know that He won't lead us wrong. I thought I'd lost in the situations in my life, but I never really lost anything. That was just the plan God used for the purpose He had for my life. It's like the reason, the season, and the lifetime, pay attention and accept whatever season a friend, family member, or even a coworker may be in and the purpose God may have them serving in your life.

Chapter Fifteen
What God Has for Me

What God has for me is for me. I don't care where you are in life, what is meant for you will be for you as well. God's plans for your life are what you have to endure. I don't care who is doing it or who starts it, if it's what He has for you, whatever it is, it's going to work in your favor. I wish I had realized that a long time ago because it would have saved me lot of heartache.

You see, I was always afraid of competition. So much so that I would stop whatever task I'd started if I felt there was too much competition involved in that task. What I did not realize was that no matter what I did, I was the authentic version of me. No one could do what God had designed me to do because He had designed me to do it.

Growing up, I'd always had the desire to have my own clothing boutique, but I was afraid because there were so many out there. Because of that, I felt that I wouldn't succeed. The crazy part was that I not only desired it, I always talked about it. I even started doing all of the research to get started, but somehow some way, I would get discouraged and wouldn't continue.

I blame myself for that intimidation because I didn't put my trust in God. I had more fear of failing than I had faith that God would allow me to succeed. I had put my trust in the things and the people I could see instead of in the God I could not see. I felt as if I didn't know enough people and because of my lack of connections, I believed the boutique wouldn't take off the way I wanted it to. So, I strayed away from my dream, but the more I began to understand who I was, the more I wondered how I could knock something without even trying it.

If it's God will, it will be successful. Success doesn't happen overnight, you have to work hard for something to become a success. A baby crawls before they walk. No matter how many times they fall, they never give up until they get it and begin to walk. This is something we learn as a child, the fundamentals of success. Anything you want to do doesn't happen overnight.

Over time I have learned that you can't always look for help from your closest friends or relatives. Oftentimes, it will be a stranger that will keep you running. I'm not saying that it's the same for everyone, but you will know who is for you and who is against you, be it friend, family member, or stranger. Just keep pushing forward and never give up. Even when you're where you want to be in life, continue to push for the highest. The sky is the limit, and if you haven't reached it, you are not yet at the limit.

Always know that faith without works is dead. Keep the faith and continue to push for your purpose. What God has for you, it is for you. You will have people that are naysayers or people that will try to make you feel you as if you aren't worthy. Know that all of God's people are worthy of anything as longs as you commit to

Him then and commit everything to Him after.

I have had people knock me down, as a result, I didn't feel as if I was worthy of anything. However, when I realized who was the head of my life and not the tail, I began to tune the negativity out one by one and things were no longer as hard as I thought. When your mind is made up and you want to win for you, it will be all so simple if you do it with God. Life is what you make it, you're the boss of your own happiness. If you want what God has for you, do what is best. Put Him first, look forward and not backwards. Leave the could have's, would have's and should have's behind and go for the prize.

Chapter Sixteen
What I Gained From It All

From everything I had gone through in my life, I gained a lot. I gained the love of God's promise for my life, I gained self-love, I gained motivation, I gained faith, and last but certainly not least, I gained my self-respect. I gained a life of being real with myself and of not hiding behind my pain.

I used to look for self-pity from others, but not many cared. And the ones that did care only cared for the moment. I was hurting in areas of my life, but I wasn't understanding the world of cruelty in which I lived. Over the course of time, I learned to stop living for others and to live for God and myself. Others would be shifted in and out of my life, those who belonged in would be shifted in and those who didn't belong would be shifted out.

You don't need people to be accepting of you, as long as you have God you have all power and all things in your hand. I gained a new relationship with God; I began to have the fire for his desire. I knew it wouldn't happen overnight, but I knew it would eventually happen because He knows my heart. At one point I only wanted Him when I was in desperate need; I was a conditional God lover. Now, I want him in every area of my life, at all times with absolutely no conditions. I have vowed that the promises He has for me will never again go unknown in my life. My faith is stronger than it has ever been.

Self-love is something I didn't have, I loved others more than I loved myself. Some people may think it is cool to love others more than you love you, but no, it's not. That's not real love. If you don't love yourself, how can you demonstrate love to another person?

Sometimes I felt that everyone in the world had to love me or even accept me. I did anything I could to prove myself to people in friendships, relationships, and in companionships. I began to motivate myself on wanting more with or without anyone. I used to feel as if I needed someone to validate me when all I really needed was me to validate me and God to validate me.

Waiting on others made me miss out on things that I should have been doing a long time ago, but I didn't have it in me to do those things, at least I thought I didn't. Now that I've learned me, no man or woman on this earth can stop me. I've made it up in my mind that I'm going to do whatever my heart desires and I'm not going to worry about who is against me. I am learning to have that crazy faith, the faith that says just do it.

Another thing I've learned through this process is that every day people do whatever it is they feel like doing. Whether it's a success or not...it gets done. They can always say, "I tried it," or "if that doesn't work, let me try it this way or let me try something different." Knowing this made me realize that we have to have faith, that crazy faith, and just do it. That's the new me. You can call me Nike because the new Simone will be just doing it. As long as I got my daddy (God), there's nothing I can't do.

My new saying for myself is, "Either you're with me or you're against me." I want to see happiness within everyone, I'm not a one sided person. The trails I have been through makes me want to see others win just as well as me. With God I now realize that I didn't live this life for me, I lived it for God's people, to motivate them to do what God has destined them to do. I never understood my journey, but I thank God that I finally leaned on his understanding and stopped trying to focus on my own. In life that is all it takes.

To this day I still try to figure people out, but I'm trying to leave that alone as well. It's not for me to figure them out. There are people that are for seasons in my life and for every situation in my life. Whether it's friends or family, everyone has place in certain situations in your life and they're there to teach you something. So, in reality you're gaining knowledge from the people around you even if they bring difficulty to your world. Some people may show you a different kind of love, a different kind of friendship, but it's on you to understand the reason they're there and their timing. And it's on you to recognize when it's their time to move on.

I gained a lot from my life learned lessons. I tried to make everyone I encountered a lifetime person when that's not what they were set out to be. Because of this, I quickly learned that you have to know the difference and let people leave or you become a victim of whatever they bring to the table once they've worn out their welcome.

Now, family is family. You will always love them, but

sometimes they have to be just that, family. You can't involve them in situations in your personal life. Like I always say, you have to know who you can talk to for what situation because some people can't handle certain things about your lifestyle. I gained a lot because of mistakes I made in this area, so, know that I understand this so much better now.

They often say that experience is a good teacher. You've got to go through to get through. Just never give up on the experience, that way you will succeed and pass the test of the lesson. The mess of it all will allow you to garner the message. You'll always win in your life, keep that in my and you will understand what you are gaining from it all.

Chapter Seventeen
Waiting on God's Promise

I had been waiting on Gods promise, a promise I thought was just passing me by. However, I had no clue that the promise was already within me. It was time I activated and tapped into God's promise for my life. Getting so caught up with all the negativity around me, I couldn't see anything God had for me. My life was consumed with any and everything except what was best for me.

I wore everybody's pain and hurt on my sleeve, but when it was my turn, I had no one there to understand what my pain was because not many people cared, especially the ones I thought would be there. When it was time to show me support, there was not of them present or accounted for. So, I continued to live as the same ole me, as if nothing ever changed. But deep inside, all I could feel was the hurt.

At this point, I felt like God had forgotten all about me. I started to do things the right way, but even my right way seemed to still lead to disaster. Just when I'd had enough and was about to give up, my life finally started to change for the better. Things started happening, people that were already destined to come into my life started appearing, and those who were no longer destined to be there started disappearing. I began to realize that God had never forgotten about me, my life was always on His time table and not on my own.

The faith that I had at that time was not as strong as I thought it should have been, but He didn't give up on me. My faith may have been limited, but I had enough of it to know that He would do what He said He would do. I never gave up on my God; I was just giving up on myself. I felt as if I couldn't do anything right, but I desperately wanted things to be right. However, through the process I came to realize that things wouldn't be right and would never be right if I didn't trust God's process.

As I said before, I had to go through everything I went through to get to God's promises. However, I took the long road. I didn't pray for His answers for my life, I lived my life the way I wanted to and prayed only after things didn't work out for me. I was the conditional prayer. Praying when things didn't go the way I thought they should have had a been a constant in my life. Had I prayed often and considered God's will when I made decisions, I would have understood the process of life a long time ago.

God's promise hasn't left you, it's there within you. You just have to go to God to find a way to tap into His promise for your life. Someone may ask how they can do that when they've been doing things their own way, or they may wonder how they can hear His answer to understand His promise. My answer to you is simple; when you're ready, give Him your undivided attention.

God will show you things through people, places, and situations, and I guarantee that even with those answers, new circumstances will arise that will still have you asking Him for answers. Why? Because we need Him, not just for one or two situations in our lives, but for every situation of our lives. However, you just have to trust Him, you just have to let go and trust Him without using your own understanding.

Become connected with His word, live through Him and not the world. To get to my promise, I had to let go of the world. I was challenged by many situations, but I had to stop letting my situations become my destination. God's promise is already within you. He is waiting on you to trust the plan and to have faith in His word and He will guide you to His promise for your life.

I will never tell you that the journey will be easy because it won't necessarily be easy. There will be times that you may even want to throw in the towel, but remember, what God has for you may not always come without difficulty. The reason for the struggle is because you can't always grow if things are effortless. How would you be able to give a testimony on what you've been through to get where you are if you never been through anything? Christians often say that there is no testimony without a test, so go through and pass the test. God's promise is waiting on you.

Chapter Eighteen
Testimony

Everything I went through was for my testimony, a testimony that was designed to help others get through. I began to learn that you don't go through just to go through. God gives His battles to His strongest people, to those He knows will use that battle to glorify Him. Some days I asked myself if I was really that strong, other times I'd get to a point where I didn't want to be strong at all. But in the end, I knew that it was not my call, so I had to adapt to what God needed me to adapt to so that I could be where I am in life today. I had to go through the pain and the discomfort to get to the purpose.

Now that I am better, I understand His plan and I finally figured out His purpose for my life. I didn't go through the pain, hurt, molestation, judgment, or through being raised without my father because I was being punished. I went through those things to be a blessing to someone else. I endured for someone who may be feeling that same pain, someone who may also be going through to help others overcome their pain and fear in life.

As people, we tend to use what we went through or are going through as a crutch, as a reason why we can't succeed in life. I was told to let my pain be my motivation, to not let it hinder me from being what God has called me to be in my life. Excuses will only hinder your growth. Rise up from it all because nothing in life is perfect.

A couple of weeks ago, I was at urgent care. I was having bad back pains and didn't know what was wrong but I wanted to check it out. I am one of those people that if I see so much as a mosquito bite I need to make sure nothing is wrong. So, I was at Memorial Urgent Care when a young lady came in to do my registration. Mind you, I was just there a couple of weeks ago with my son. I never carried my married name, I always used my maiden name, but for some reason she couldn't find me in their system.

The young lady went to ask for my ID which has my married name hyphenated on it.

She then said, "This why I can't find you, you changed your name."

I told her that I was divorced and had never used the name for my insurance. She began to tell me how sorry she was about my divorce.

I looked up at her and I said, "Don't be sorry, what God has planned for me is what I'm waiting on. My divorce wasn't a sorry situation, my marriage had just had run its course."

This young woman then began to tell me about her relationship with her child's father, a man she'd been with for a while. But he hadn't married her; he'd taken another woman's hand in marriage. However, they were still "kicking it". That was when I knew that God was using me at that moment. I began to speak to her, I opened up to her about my own life and told her that she deserved so much better.

I said, "Never become someone's second place when you should be number one. Obviously you weren't the chosen one in his life, so stop giving him what he wants because he didn't give you what you wanted. As long as you keep kicking it with him, he is winning and you're still losing. The bottom line is that you were hurting yourself thinking that he loved you while he went off and married someone else. Never position yourself to please someone else and hurt you just to satisfy their needs while sacrificing your happiness. It will never work."

I explained to her that she should let him go.

"You are beautiful," I said to her. "You have potential, and you are doing great things for yourself and your son. Never let your son see that you are weak and settling. What he needs to see is a strong woman who wants the best for herself."

One thing we all have to realize is that kids are not dumb or crazy, they watch our every move. They don't want to see us hurting. I do not care if we're with their other parent or not, getting out of an unhealthy relationship is called happiness and self-respect. I continued talking to her, telling her that she was demonstrating weakness for a man's pleasure because there was no way she could've been happy being the side chick when she felt she should have been the wife.

She replied by asking, "But why is he still coming to me when he's already married?"

She was basically telling me that he didn't really want the wife because he kept coming back to her.

My response was to the point. "No, baby. He is a man and he is winning. If he wanted you, he would have married you. He got what he wanted; you were just convenient to him. I know this because I've been there; the only difference is that I was the wife. He came and went, but still stayed where he said he wanted to be. Had I not stopped it, I'd still be stuck trying to figure out why."

Sometimes men are confusing, but we help with the confusion when we allow them to use us the way they want to use us. Ladies, it's time to stop selling yourselves short for their pleasure. If marriage is something they want, whether it's with you or not, make them live up to it. Don't help them cheat, make them honor their vows by not being that second chick in line. That woman really had me going, I was talking to her like I'd known her for years. I was on fire, not realizing that at that moment I was stepping into my purpose.

The moral of this story is that I didn't even realize I was ministering to this young lady until I finished. She hugged me so tightly and thanked me so much for speaking to her. She was telling me that someone had already told her things similar to what I had just told her, and she felt that she just gotten confirmation from me. If someone says that to you, those words should let you know that God is using you even when you don't think you're ready. He starts you off with just a taste and then he fills you up with the full coarse meal.

I knew that day that QSB, Queens Stay Busy, was ready to launch. QSB is an organization for women and men to understand their purpose in life and to lean on God's understanding and not their own understanding.

Never stop reaching for the best, stay motivated to do more in life. Never quit, and know that it doesn't end with what you went through, what you went through is only the beginning. Right now, I'm an open book. Prior to my journey and also through some stages of it, I used to hide all my pain and I wore it so well that you would never understand how I did it. Sometimes I ask myself how did I did it, but at the end of it all I realized that it was nothing but God.

I still go through, but I've learned to trust God and to keep pushing. Where I am in life now, I can handle it way better than I used too. I share my testimony and my experience with whomever is in need of hearing it. It wasn't given to me to hide it, it was given to me for a purpose.

My current job has me working with the public in the medical field. I often find myself speaking Gods Word to them because they're coming in with all types of pains and issues. You would think it's just medical help that I give, but no, it's not just medical. I have patients that come with a story, patients that I actually pray for and I do it because it's the right thing to do. But all the while, I'm talking and speaking of how God Good is, and of how they need to give it to Him because doctors or surgeons can tell them anything, but God has the last say.

I am just realizing that God had been using me the whole time. God has His way of showing you who He is and what His plans are for you. While you're waiting in the midst of your storm, He is already using you.

When I started writing this book, I was still searching for my purpose and my plan for my life. I even stopped writing, praying for God to send me the message that I needed to write. I made up every excuse that I could think of about why I needed to stop writing because I felt as if I still hadn't heard from God. However, what I began to learn in the process was that He was already speaking, I just wasn't listening.

I went on a fast and still nothing. I remember telling my coworker that I knew what I wanted to do, I knew the desire of my heart, but I had not been cleared by God to do it. I told her I that I was going to do this fast and I was going to listen for God. But during all that time I was steady mentoring to all that were around me. I just didn't get it. Thank God that I finally got it.

QSB, *Queens Stay Busy*, is in process and will be launched right along with this book.

Thank You Jesus

Conclusion

The moral of my story is that you should understand your pain because eventually it will lead you to your purpose. God has a way of showing you His purpose and without God you will never get there. Your life is not just about you. Always remember the life you are living is set up to inspire someone else's life. Again, it is said that God gives His battles to His strongest people, trust the process, don't fold, and everything will work out for your good. It took me a while to get that, but I understand it now.

My life has done a complete one-eighty since I decided to get connected with God and build the relationship I needed with Him. I'm engaged to be married in 2019. My kids are happy and seeing me happy has made them more supportive than ever. Kamitra, Destiny, and Wayne, you three are the reason I pushed and did it all. You guys are my rock. Carlos Johnson, my soon to be husband, I love you and thank you from the bottom of my heart for being just you to me.

Finding Your Purpose in Your Pain
THE WORK BOOK

I hope my story encourages, inspires and drives you to want to seek out and find the purpose in your pain. I want to help you in your search by guiding you with specific questions that will push and pull you, cause you to dig up old dirt, and open wounds that are only healed on the surface but are infected underneath.

Through the next three sections you will revisit your past, review your present, and become renewed for your future. I ask that you be honest with yourself. No one will see the answers. They are specifically asked to help you see that what was is not what is and what is, is not what will be. If you can't be honest with anyone else, you must be honest with yourself. And if you can be honest with yourself, you can be honest with God.

The Past Me

the *Past* – Definition: (adjective)

1.   No longer current; gone by; over

2.   Having existed or occurred in an earlier time; bygone

1.   Often, we encounter people, places and things that shape our future that we currently living. What in your past, no matter the length of time, has shaped your NOW? What is it about that 'moment' that has caused a reaction that negatively impact you in this day?

_____

_____

_____

_____

_____

_____

_____

_____

_____

_____

_____

_____

_____

_____

_____

_____

_____

_____

_____

_____

_____

_____

_____

2.   Who, from your past, has influenced you the most? How is this person's influence, teaching and/or guidance reflected in your present day and why?

_____

_____

_____

_____

_____

_____

_____

_____

_____

_____

_____

_____

_____

_____

_____

_____

_____

_____

_____

_____

_____

_____

_____

_____

_____

_____

_____

_____

_____

_____

_____

_____

_____

_____

3.   What do you think God was teaching you, in your past, that you weren't aware at the time?

_____
_____
_____
_____
_____
_____
_____
_____
_____
_____
_____
_____
_____
_____
_____
_____
_____
_____
_____
_____
_____
_____
_____
_____

_____

_____

_____

_____

_____

_____

_____

_____

_____

_____

4.   Write a prayer concerning your <u>past</u>. Seek God to deliver you
from what has had you bound from far too long. Refer to Scripture to
write this prayer. Declare Gods word over your life.

_____

_____

_____

_____

_____

_____

_____

_____

The Present Me

the *Present* – Definition: (adjective)

1. Being, existing, or occurring at this time or now; current

2. At this time; at hand; immediate

1. What do you need to remove from your thought life to see the purpose in your pain?

_____

_____

_____

_____

_____

_____

_____

_____

_____

_____

_____

_____

_____

_____

_____

_____

_____

_____

_____

_____

_____

_____

_____

_____

_____

_____

_____

_____

_____

_____

_____

_____

_____

_____

_____

_____

_____

_____

_____

_____

2.   What is holding you back from becoming the woman or man God has called you to be?

_____

_____

_____

_____

_____

_____

_____

_____

- Write a plan to counteract what is holding you back. What can you do to push pass that hold, to break through it?

_____

_____

_____

_____

_____

_____

_____

_____

_____

_____

_____

3.   <u>Finding the Purpose in Your Pain</u>

- Take a blank piece of paper, make 3 columns and follow these instructions:

    1.   Make a list of things that have <u>caused</u> great pain in your life

    2.   Next, make a list of how you felt and <u>still feel</u> from those moments

    3.   Finally, make a list of why you think those things <u>happened</u>.

- As you review your list, pray for an understand for Gods purpose in each one of them. As you await the answer, write down what you learned from each experience. This will take some deep thought and being truthful with oneself. Even if the pain was great, there was a lesson for you to have learned.

4. Write a prayer concerning your <u>present.</u> List everything the first list declaring you are free from PAIN so you can walk in, and understand your purpose. Refer to Scripture to write this prayer. Declare Gods word over your life.

_____

_____

_____

_____

_____

_____

_____

_____

_____

_____

_____

_____

_____

_____

_____

_____

_____

_____

_____

The Future Me

the *Future* – Definition: (noun)

1. Time that is to be or come hereafter

2. Something that will exist or happen in time to come

1. What are three major desires/hopes you have in God and why?

1) _____

_____

_____

_____

_____

_____

2) _____

_____

_____

_____

_____

_____

3) _____

_____

_____

_____

_____

_____

2.   Describe your current relationship. Is it healthy or unhealthy, leading to or has led to marriage, is it new or seasoned? Do you feel wanted, desired, needed, appreciated in your relationship? When you think of your relationship, does positive thoughts come to mind or negative?

_____

_____

_____

_____

_____

_____

_____

_____

_____

_____

_____

_____

_____

_____

_____

_____

_____

_____

_____

_____

_____

_____

_____

3.   Habakkuk 2:2-3, *And the Lord answered me: 'Write the vision; make it plain on tablets, so he may run who reads it. For still the vision awaits its appointed time; it hasten to the end-it will not lie."*

I want to challenge you to write a letter to yourself dated five years from now, addressed to Dear Future Me. After you write it, seal it up and put it in a safe place. When the date comes, read it to see if you have a stood up to the vision you had for your life.

4.   Write a prayer concerning your future. Include the hopes for yourself and family. Refer to Scripture to write this prayer. Declare Gods word over your life.

_____

_____

_____

_____

_____

_____

_____

_____

_____

_____

_____

_____

_____

_____

_____

_____

_____

_____

_____

_____

_____

Decide TODAY to walk in your purpose and work on your it instead of carrying your pain. Remember, YOUR PAIN IS YOUR PURPOSE

MY PAIN IS MY PURPOSE

Bonus
Material

TABLE OF CONTENTS

By Toyonda Simone
Author | CEO

ELEVATING

Queen, never stop elevating yourself to that next level of your life. No matter what obstacles life may bring continue to press your way through. There will be major distractions that you will face from every angle. That's when you must put the armor of God on and continue to keep elevating. No one or nothing can stop you from being great; elevation is your key to success. What God has for you it is for you. Know your purpose, push hard, and having faith. Trust and believe it will not go unnoticed. Amazing work will come to light. Take time out for you. Focus on what's around you and what can elevate you. It's not an easy task but prayer will help you through and trust God with your vision to help you become better. You will face competitors, naysayers, and even disbelievers, but once you are aware of how authentic you are who gone stop you? We see this every day...there are plenty of business offering same service or product, but they have a specialty to their brand. Making it unique in its own way. These entrepreneurs stuck to their dreams and became successful with the help of strangers who supported their dream and vision. Once you become familiar with your purpose continue to elevate for better.

Did you know God wants all his children to have riches both of knowledge and wisdom? Romans 11:33-36 gives you the word of how God wants His people to manifest. There will be bumps and bruises during this process but don't let it get you down or even discourage you. Let it be your motivation for the next level. A man may tell you "NO" but the God I serve can change that "NO" into something courageous in the right situation. Never let "NO" discourage you because it just means that God has a greater plan for your purpose. I am that *victim* that doubted myself in a lot of dreams and vision I once had but never pursued. I would start but always listening to other opinions, I would become discouraged and would not continue. Missing the support that was needed and my faith not strong enough, I became scared of competition, perception, and even feeling unworthy of myself. It's time to live your life and pursuing your dreams. Supporting others and their vision is fine but don't leave yours behind.

Queen, grab your bag and elevate yourself to the next level.

BEING BOLD

Queen, never be afraid of what God has for you. God's plan for your life may seem to become a bit uncomfortable at times but that's the glory of it. Tackling something that is unfamiliar to you allows you to challenge yourself. A challenge is something some can adapt, and some can't but every situation you are put in is part of God 's plan. He knows how much and what you can handle. Don't fold or bend in the process. Instead, push for greatness. Have that crazy faith. "God, I don't know what I'm doing but You gave me this task and I'm going to depend on You to pull me through." You have to talk to God like you would talk to anyone else. He is listening. Be bold and do what you are called to do with trusting Gods promise for your life. You are a child of God and He will not leave you nor forsake you through the *Being Bold* process. No one or nothing can come between God's plan for your life. *Being Bold* is believing, trusting the process and following your heart.

Queen, it may not look good at the beginning, but you will continue the journey and your breakthrough will come. *Being*

Bold can help you in your personal relationship, work relationship, and business relationship. When God is moving on your behalf you may begin to question the process because it does not seem familiar. It's okay to feel scared. Pray about it, continue to push and you won't go wrong. Anything God is a part of it will result in greatness. Dream big! Create your dream, give it back to God and He will help you through every step. Don't stress about the support...it will come. God will surround you with the right people at the right time that are made for your journey.

Motivating Herself

Queen, stay motivated within yourself. Pray and talk to God to help keep a clear mind. You will have people in your life whose only purpose is to distract you. Continue to have a connection with God to keep your spirits up and depend on God words. It's plenty of times I felt down and drained because I didn't see the process. I can recall giving up and throwing in the towel, but I had to remember what my purpose was, so I can look forward and know there will be better days ahead. Your purpose is not just for you. It is also to help others who have been where you've been or in a situation right now and needs to motivation to help them get through what you've already been through. When you remember that and remember how you felt during your time of need that should be your number one reason to keep motivating yourself to stay busy in the process. You should always want to motivate others for the best in life just as well as yourself. Begin speaking positively over your life, speak to God tell Him your desires and He will provide them to you. In Psalms 37:4 it states, "Take delight in the Lord, and He will give you the desires of your heart." If we live by His words we will have a successful life. There will be many bumps and bruises but keep yourself motivated by His word and follow your heart. Don't worry about people negativity. Man has a way of letting you down. Be a motivation within yourself.

FAILING FORWARD

Queen, let your failure be your motivation. It's nothing like learning from your own mistakes. The experience is the best teacher. When you fail at what you did wrong, it is impossible to make the same mistake unless you're just not focused. When you fail at something in life it gives you more motivation to want to get back up and try again. Don't settle for failure. Instead learn from failure you. Whatever you do pray about it and be about it. s long as it is God's will, it will work in your favor. Just because you failed at it doesn't meant to be. It could mean it wasn't done the right way God intended. We intend to do things our way expect it to work but seeking the will of God guarantees it will work. Always let your failure be your motivation. Never look at it as a disappointment. Instead look at it as a step forward. We are not made perfect, but we can work on being a greater person.

I failed at a lot of things in life. If I let that be a response to my life I would not be here trying to motivate you to stay busy as a Queen. Life will always make us feel like all we can do is fail but the love of God will ensure failing is just a test to see how you well we would handle the test. Once you overcome failure I dare you to try it God's way and let us see what happens. Make that test your testimony. *Failing Forward* is what make you hungry for better.

BEING IMPEFECT

Queen, never feel like you can't fail. If you don't fail how can you understand the success? If you don't fail how can you appreciate the test? The answer to both of those questions you can't understands or appreciate the outcome. If everything was perfect there will be no test for the testimony God is setting you up for. Life was never made to be easy. We go through everything for a reason. Had I not gone through the disappointment and failure in my life I wouldn't be able to fulfill my purpose for God. Being imperfect is what God want from us. We have to experience life in order to understand His promise. If I go through nothing how can I appreciate something? Be ready for whatever challenge comes your way.

Let us just think for a moment if we were all perfect how could we believe or even depend on the word of God? Honestly, I believe we will not need the word of God if we were so perfect. We are imperfect and sinners for a reason. We must appreciate life itself. You can't appreciate something if you haven't been through anything. How can I sit before you and tell you how to be true to the word of God, if I don't know what is or what it means to be true to the word of God? When you have a testimony, you have lived to understand that His word is your truth. So, it is quite okay not to be perfect in His eyes, which is the eyes that matter. Being Imperfect is what make you better physically, mentally and successfully.

BEING EMPOWERED

Queen, knowing that all power is within you must stay connected and continue to pray. Your prayers and connection with God will never go unnoticed. You may sit and pray, waiting for His answers but don't always seem to hear Him when you want. Don't get discouraged. Stay connected and committed so you can hear what His plan is for you. Be ready to listen and accept the unknown.

God reveals himself to you in so many ways, but you may get so caught up in the moment that you miss your own answer to your prayers. It's all in the power of you to know when God is revealing Himself to you. Take time out and just listen and embracing His presents.

EMBRACING THE PROCESS

Queen, knowing failure is part of the process, will eliminate the delay of the process. Embrace whatever comes with success. Embrace that everything may not come easy, things will happen. By understanding that what God has for you it is for you. When it's God timing it's your timing, God will give you everything your heart desires only if it's part of His plans for your life. You will begin to recognize that the road won't be easy, and that failure is part of the growth. Embrace the process of your journey. Having faith in whatever you do in your personal life, business life and spiritual life is a sign of embracing the process. One thing I leave with you do not give up on your purpose. If it's your purpose and it's God's plan for your life, God will see you though.

Embrace the process!!!

Conclusion

These 7 ways I have presented to you are 7 ways a Queen should stay busy. Your situation is not your destination, use every aspect to grow within yourself. Its ok to be everything to everyone else but be that by putting yourself first. Everyone has a purpose in life tap into your purpose and understand your purpose by being connected with God to fulfill his plans for your life. Queens, I encourage you to grab your bags and stay busy. Be that boss, entrepreneur or whatever your calling is to fulfill God purpose for your life. Fulfilling Gods purpose become the most amazing work you could have ever accomplish.

Know your purpose and understand His plan

ABOUT THE AUTHOR

Toyonda Simone is a Motivational Speaker, Entrepreneur, Life Coach, the Founder of Queens Stay Busy and the CEO of KD_KreativeDesign Boutique as well as KD Beauty Makeup. Her mission is to empower women to stay busy chasing their dreams and to manifest and reflect the queen within! Toyonda believes the life that God has given us has a purpose and having faith in Him will lead us to our destiny. She wants to see all women operating in faith, forgiveness, and freedom.

Connect with her on social media:

Website: http://www.ToyondaSimone.com

Facebook: ToyondaSimone

Instagram: ToyondaSimone

_____

www.ingramcontent.com/pod-product-compliance
Lightning Source LLC
Chambersburg PA
CBHW071121090426
42736CB00012B/1978

My Pain is MY PURPOSE

There is a popular gospel song by William McDowell that sings, "My life is not my own. To You I belong. In those words, are the truth that many have failed to accept: *My life is not my own. It belongs to God.* Because of this fact, God will proceed to use your life, from birth to death, as a tool to be used for His will and purpose.

Although life can be hard yet joyful, trying yet full of hope when we embrace the simple concept that He is using us for a greater purpose, victories and defeat begin to make sense. Toyonda Simone opens old wounds, reveals the deepness of who she is and shows you the power of God just to find the reason for everything that YOU had to endure.

My Pain is My Purpose explores one woman's life with and without God. Journey with Toyonda Simone a she finds the purpose in her pain and receive the greater things of God. At the end, you will be encouraged, inspired and ready to search out and find the purpose in your pain.

Toyonda Simone is a Motivational Speaker, Entrepreneur Life Coach, the Founder of Queens Stay Busy and the CEC of KD_KreativeDesign Boutique as well as KD Beauty Makeup. Her mission is to empower women to stay busy chasing their dreams and to manifest and reflect the queen within! Toyonda believes the life that God has given us has a purpose and having faith in Him will lead us to our destiny. She wants to see all women operating in faith, forgiveness, and freedom.

CONNECT WITH HER ON SOCIAL MEDIA:
WEBSITE: WWW.TOYONDASIMONE.COM
FACEBOOK: TOYONDASIMONE
INSTAGRAM: TOYONDASIMONE

ISBN 9780692101353

90000

9 780692 101353